HOW TO MAKE
BLOCKBUSTER
MOVIE TRAILERS

TOM GETTY

ACROLIGHT
PICTURES
LLC

Acrolight Pictures

An imprint of Acrolight Pictures *LLC*

THIS IS AN ACROLIGHT PICTURES LLC BOOK
PUBLISHED BY TOM GETTY

Copyright © 2022 Acrolight Pictures LLC

This edition published 2022 by Acrolight Pictures LLC.

Press, Johnstown, Pennsylvania

LCCN: 2022909381
ISBN: 978-0-9974800-5-4

Designed by Tom Getty

FIRST EDITION

To Robert V. Crites
For support, scholarship, and inspiration

Contents

ACKNOWLEDGEMENTS

The following pages are the work of one author, but they are also the result of many people, and many lucky breaks. There are many people to thank.

My mother, Sally Hare Getty, for encouragement and support during the writing of this book.

My father, Charles A. Getty, for encouragement, support, and listening to rough drafts of this book. As well, for reviewing and enjoying the trailers I've made.

My sister, Colleen Hepler, for encouragement, support, and many talks on the phone.

My brother-in-law, Jeremy Hepler, for encouragement and support.

Ginger Stepp, for consultation, encouragement, and support.

Galen Christy of High Octane Pictures, for giving me my break in making movie trailers; for constant encouragement and, of course, keeping me in the game.

Greg Loscar, CBS's leading, Emmy-Award-winning, promotions-man, for teaching me promotions, that the dialogue goes first, and for much, much patience for someone very green.

Samantha Richardson, for opportunity, and patience.

All these people and more had more than a hand in creating the pages that follow.

A note on pronouns:
Every other chapter is male; every other chapter is female.

INTRODUCTION

Over 700 films were released in 2019, according to the Motion Picture Association of America—roughly 150 more than 2010. In less than a decade, there were 30% *more* movies *each* year. To put in perspective: by 2030, a thousand new movies each year will flood the market. That's just for movies that obtain a rating from the Motion Pictures Association of America. The numbers do not account for the "indie" titles that overwhelm the festivals each year. For instance, the Sundance Film festival, alone, each year, receives over 3,000 feature film submissions. But that pales in comparison to the amount released *on the internet*. Each year, Netflix, Amazon, Hulu releases hundreds of films, TV series, documentaries, pushing the total haul into the thousands. Never mind YouTube, where millions of users upload 500 hours of video per minute—every minute. Hour after hour. That's 30,000 hours, per hour. All of it, ostensibly, for free.

The filmmaker, the producer, the movie-executive looks at those numbers with a lump in his throat. Quickly, he tries to rationalize: most of those movies, movie-media, cannot possibly be any good. The producer would be right. Most of what is released, most of what is uploaded, is bad. Subjectivity not withstanding—and, as the reader will see, having absolutely nothing to do with anything—most of what is released each year is bad, is poorly done, is not deserving of any attention. From the backyard production to the most expensive film in Hollywood—most of it is undisciplined jettison. The filmmaker, the producer, the executive, can safely assume 99.9% of what is released will disappoint whoever consumes it.

But, that does not matter.

Movies—video-media, content, films, however one puts it—are temporal. Their consumption requires time. Their digestion requires even more. It takes experience to find out something is bad or good. And even at that, no one really knows. All those movies, irrespective of their quality, require a consumption not of themselves—but of time.

The competition is not against those movies. It's against the *tens of thousands of hours* those movies themselves individually command in attention. Which, when tabulated, would require over a single year of constant viewing just to get through. Five thousand movies would equate to, roughly, *10,000 hours of film*. That's 400 days of straight viewing.

And by then, there would still be more, newer movies to sit through, to sift about, to digest.

It would literally never end.

Simply, a movie cannot compete on quality. It is a meaningless qualifier that will never be discovered or understood. It is an afterthought.

The War of Hollywood

A movie must compete on time. The competition of Hollywood, of entertainment, is not a battle for attention, money, fame, or power. It is a war for time.

And time, is non-negotiable.

The box office is not a reflection of dollars earned, but of time spent. The top films dominated not just money—although, the coffers certainly suggest that—but rather, and more importantly, time. When the latest AVENGERS sequel tops the box office, it is not a reflection of just money spent, but of time invested. Which is a far greater investment when one considers how limited the hours of our lives are. Simply, box office success reflects how people wanted to spend their leisure—for better or worse.

When it comes to movie success—money is not the problem. Time is. Money is only the prize; time is the battleground.

It is for this reason movie trailers are so dynamic. They are short. They are a compression of what may be. If trailers didn't exist, they would have to be invented. There is a reason they evolved right along with Hollywood. They save time. Movies are amorphous, opaque, unquantifiable bloats—they might as well all be bad. Trailers are direct, punctual, qualifiable propositions. They are helpful sales letters on the route to quality entertainment.

A Definition of Trailers

But what is a trailer? How is it defined? It is taken for granted in the industry that a movie trailer is a commercial, an advertisement, for a film that is to be released in the future. Indeed, the word "trailer" is unfortunate. It originated because previews, these mini movies, at one point in time, played *after* the main feature. They *trailed*, as it were, the film reel of the main feature. Somehow, it stuck with movie people; now movie previews are ubiquitously referred to as "trailers."

As a result, the word "trailer," outside the industry, gives off the wrong impression. Ask any normal person what a trailer is, and they will assume it's something they see on the highway, trailing behind a utility truck. It certainly does not reflect any of the glamour or prestige of future entertainment.

The word "trailer," for most people, evokes completely different concepts.

But what concept is it supposed to evoke? A clip show? A highlight reel? A commercial? A montage? What, after all, is a preview of coming attractions?

It is a concept that has developed surreptitiously. In 1913, publicist Nils Thor Granlund produced the first trailer by showing rehearsal footage for an upcoming musical called *The Pleasure Seekers*. It was enough to simply show footage related to the coming attraction. The practice grew to using footage from the actual movie; then introduced copy, music, and ultimately, dialogue. In 1927, with the words, "Ladies and gentlemen," THE JAZZ SINGER was the first movie trailer to sell its wares with recorded voice. The first instinct was for that voice to call THE JAZZ SINGER one of the year's most "outstanding pictures."

The Actual Business of Entertainment

From the beginning, trailers were made to signal the existence of a movie. They were created because they needed to be. The filmmakers, the stars, the producers, the executives, everyone involved, even way back then, understood this simple tenet: Movies do not succeed based on the movies themselves. They need promotion. They need trailers.

Movies succeed because of promotion.

As in all fields, the product is secondary; it is promotion that takes center stage. When a movie takes off in its opening weekend at the box office, it is because of the promotion of that movie. A film is not rewarded for its quality. It is rewarded for the quality of its marketing. That a film "grows legs" through "word of mouth" is just another extension of effective marketing. The film had a message, it resonated with ticket buyers; the filmgoer became the film's promoter. When a movie does well with word of mouth, it is due to publicity. Word of mouth is little more than the filmgoer picking up where the promoter left off. In the case of word-of-mouth, the people are doing the promoting.

Entertainment is a promotion business, not a moviemaking one.

Each year, Hollywood spends more and more money on making movies. In 2019, Hollywood spent $65 billion (Navarro, 2021). But, in that same year, they only shelled out a little under one billion for advertising (Guttmann, 2021). A comparatively small amount. Year after year, Hollywood wastes more resources than necessary on making movies, overlooking one single fact: **People pay to see a movie. Not to have seen it.**

The trailer brings in the money. Not the film.

Without trailers, all movies would perish upon release. Those thousands of new films would cannibalize each other into oblivion; audiences would simply give up out of confusion. The world of film would concentrate around a blurry composite, a veritable trash-heap of camouflaged cinema, a veiled, errant haze of which only the most idle would dare penetrate.

Without trailers, Hollywood would cease to exist.

For a movie to have any kind of chance, it requires a well-oiled, highly refined movie trailer. There's no other way. It is only through a trailer that a movie does any kind of speaking to any kind of public. It is only through the trailer that a movie communicates its existence, entices, and directs.

The majority of conversation about a film centers around its trailer.

In the days when there were fewer movies, people had time to—indeed, were forced to—take in and actually digest a movie. Discussion centered around whether a movie was bad or good. Now, that kind of discussion is reserved for the limited few movies that break through the clutter, if that. Conversation today, for the vast majority of films, centers around the trailer—and only the trailer. Whether it's a good trailer, a bad trailer, whether it reveals too much, or too little, whether the movie "looks" good, or whether it "looks" bad. Film commerce has long since passed the era of the film-as-king, the film-as-event. Today, it is all about the trailer. The trailer is the content.

The trailer is king.

Making one, however, is all together a different matter.

What Trailers Actually Are

When a filmmaker sets out to make a trailer, he will confront a sizable wall. If he is honest with himself, there will be great tension. Of course, not all filmmakers, producers, and executives are honest with themselves. Especially the filmmaker. He will believe that the trailer is something that can be artistically assembled over the weekend, with a few trailer worthy shots here, a few creative edits there, and some music for exciting measure. He will believe that the trailer—his trailer—is an artful showcase of a movie well done.

It is no such thing.

A trailer deploys sales techniques, not artistic merit.

Of course, artistic design is crucial. But it is even more crucial the trailer's artistic design be wrapped around expert salesmanship. This salesmanship motivated by age-old principles of attention, interest, desire, and action. The mark of a good trailer is its ability to do what any sales-literature does for its product—direct attention, garner interest, conjure desire, and motivate action. That is the formula. Sales are the main concern—not artistic expression, not artistic *reception*. Trailers can be art, but they must never be art in and of themselves. A good trailer sells. A bad trailer does nothing but squawk and make noise.

A trailer promotes, it does not entertain.

While some people might derive a great deal of entertainment out of watching movie trailers, that should never confuse the purpose of a trailer. Everything in the design of a trailer should be done so through the purpose of promotion. Too often trailers try to entertain, bemuse, amuse, delight. They are to inform, educate, direct, stimulate. Trailers are best when their intent is to persuade, not to fascinate. The orientation is about selling movie tickets, not entertaining an audience. The trailer must be seen as a promotional tool.

A trailer directs attention, it does not get it.

For a trailer to simply clamber for attention is not enough. It must get attention, and then direct that attention in some fashion. Too often trailers just aim to garner recognition; they do nothing with it. Urgency and direction are needed. A trailer must say, "Look here, look there." Not, "Look at me, look at me."

A trailer creates expectation, not curiosity.

To simply arouse curiosity is not enough. Expectation must be created. The difference between the two being that curiosity is idle bemusement; expectation excites, directs. A trailer has to triangulate desire to see a film by arousing concrete expectations; expectations that demand fulfillment; fulfillment only possible by viewing the actual motion picture. A good trailer places expectations in the mind of the viewer; it does not beat them over the head with sound and noise. Expectation stimulates the imagination. Movie trailers project in the mind just as much as they do on screen.

A trailer sells story, not mystery.

The audience wants information, not intrigue. They need that information to build a model in their mind of what the story *will be*—spoilers and all. Simply, a film cannot exist without some sort of prior positioning. Not only is a trailer a tool of promotion, but it's also the means by which audiences form expectations about the film they're about to watch. If movies were sold 100% on mystery, there would be no need for trailers (or movies themselves). Audiences would simply go to the multiplex, then, based on just the title, pick a film at random. This would lead to a lot of frustrated patrons. Quality trailers instill anticipation; selling story instills that anticipation.

There is nothing more complicated in entertainment than producing a movie trailer. Maybe writing a script. Maybe editing a film. But unlike either one of those, little has been written or explained on how to make a trailer. It's one of the few remaining dark arts of moviemaking.

A Framework in Making Trailers

In the following pages, *How To Make Blockbuster Trailers* aims to demonstrate the creation of movie trailers—from the ground up, from scratch. Whether the trailer producer is working on a multi-million-dollar blockbuster, or a no-budget thesis, this book will guide the aspiring trailer producer in coming up with an appeal, arranging the building blocks of that appeal, finding its underlying structure, creating music and sound, editing everything together, mixing and mastering, and finally, launching the trailer out into and beyond the cluttered world of film media.

Chapter 1, "The Universal Appeal," examines what it means to come up with a compelling appeal. Simply, what is it about movies—universally—that motivates people to attend them? Once the question is answered, once an appeal is understood, the real trailer work can begin. Chapter 2, "Selling Story," shows how to arrange the most fundamental aspects of a trailer: its dialogue. Chapter 3, "A Trailer's Rhythm," looks at how to establish a trailer's rhythm. It also asks which comes first: sound or music? The question will be answered. Chapter 4, "Music Design," is about how to create music—even if the trailer producer is not a musician. Chapter 5, "Sound Design," dives deep into the production of sound design in a trailer, deciphering which sound effects to use, how they relate, and what categories they fall into. Chapter 6, "Editing," instructs on finding the right "trailer worthy" shots, how to categorize them, and what to do with them once arranged. Chapter 7, "Copywriting," explains the art of copywriting and how it is essential to create effective taglines. Then, Chapter 8, "Title Design," shows how to take that copywriting, that sales literature, and arrange it into aesthetically pleasing and beautiful titles. Chapter 9, "Mixing," delves into the art of mixing; how to achieve the right balance between dialogue, sound effects, and music. Chapter 10, "Mastering," investigates the art of mastering; how to combine the mix all into a singular, broadcast-ready, competitive audio track. Chapter 11, "Marketing" covers what to do with a trailer once it has been made, how to get it out there, and how to effectively market it. Chapter 12, "A New Method" talks about a revolutionary approach to not just trailer design, but to moviemaking as a whole. Simply, it is all about doing the trailer first—not last; before the film is ever shot.

The following pages aim to provide a framework on making movie trailers, to guide future filmmakers, producers, movie executives, in making these very important sales presentations. This book is about how to make blockbuster movie trailers. Not just movie trailers—but *blockbuster* movie trailers. The kind of trailers you see in theaters. The kind of trailers that aim to persuade and persuade in large quantities.

This is a book on how to make movie trailers that compete. This is a book on how to make movie trailers that direct attention.

This is a book on how to make movie trailers that *sell*.

1

THE UNIVERSAL APPEAL

Motivations & Appeals

The hardest job the trailer producer will face when making a trailer is coming up with an appeal. Indeed, "what" is being sold when selling a movie? This is not an easy question. And made no easier by the various influences that go into making a trailer. Everyone will have different ideas. The executive was moved to share a vision with the world. The film, made by other filmmakers, was motivated by a competing vision—and it's always a competing vision. The audience, spending money on tickets, is motivated by the desire to be entertained, and to be entertained in the way they want to be entertained. All three of them are involved in the same conspiracy. The executive believes that what was a hit yesterday, will be tomorrow. She does this because of the box office numbers. The filmmaker, inspired by countless movies, can only ever make a movie based on what she already knows—other movies. The audience, on the other hand, is dealing with its own nostalgic crisis. While the executive is typically concerned with financial inspirations, the audience has a similar, while inversely, informed hope: they want more of what moved them yesterday. It is a safe bet. Like executives, audiences as well must invest time and money, and can only make those investments based on what has already happened. It is all those audiences know. It is all they can know. And because executive, filmmaker, and audience can only ever try to understand what the other wants, because these three forces can never, realistically align, these combined forces are characterized, typified, powered, reasoned through, built up, by making assumptions. The executives can only guess what will work, as she is working toward a future goal; the filmmakers can only make such a good movie; and the audience—that amorphous blob that has yet to uniquely assemble en masse and buy tickets for the present film—has yet to vocalize, or prove, what it is they want. They are not sure and will not be until the movie is over. Therefore, as legendary screenwriter William Goldman once said about the industry: "No one knows nothing."

But the trailer producer must know. Because at the confluence of these inspirations is where the trailer producer will find herself. A trailer must be produced; and it must be produced with accuracy, devoid of any inspiration beyond what is potentially unifying these three forces. The trailer producer must do so through creative action; by assembling dialogue, selecting music, selecting rhythm, curating edits, writing effective copy, designing eye-catching titles, mixing, mastering, and delivering. The trailer producer must do this work through the powers-that-be, by working with the film that is available, and then somehow by harnessing and translating the two, hoping to meet the third, the audience—who want something, but are, as of yet, unwilling to share what those wants are. Simply, the trailer producer must triangulate competing desires into a competitive and motivating two minutes of cinema. Because ultimately, it is through the trailer producer where all effective pressures of moviemaking—and *moviegoing*—converge. It is up to—and usually left to—the trailer producer to sell the motion picture to the moviegoing public. Herculean in nature, the task involves corralling up all available energies behind the movie and funneling them through a sales process; everyone, all the while, hoping that success will be on the other end. No small feat. But it must be done; and it must be understood.

While everyone can miss the point, the trailer producer must catch the boat. She must have a deep understanding of what she is attempting to do. She must know exactly what her aim has to be. Because what is being sold in a trailer? A movie? An experience? An actor? Entertainment? Fun? Horror? Action? Suspense? To whom, and where? And why would they be interested in what is being sold? It is up to the trailer producer to not only know these answers, but to do so with a global scope. She must know what is behind the executive's ideas. She must know what is behind the—as of now—concrete nature of the film's very existence (a finished film is a finished film; no amount of money can change that). She must know what will then be appealing about that film, so that she can share that, and the enthusiasm *for it*, with the world.

A trailer producer must understand exactly what is motivating everyone involved when it comes to moviemaking, and moviegoing.

First, she must consider the executive. What motivates her? The art? The money? Both? It is hard to say. While one would think money, that is not always the case. Some executives genuinely love movies. Otherwise, they would be selling some other commodity. A better question would be, "What does she base her decisions on?" Again, the past is looked to. More specifically, and more rationally, the box office. The grosses of past films. The most obvious list to consult is the top ten highest grossing of all time.

1) Avatar — $2,845,899,541
2) Avengers: Endgame — $2,797,800,564
3) Titanic — $2,207,986,545
4) Star Wars Ep. VII: The Force Awakens — $2,064,615,817
5) Avengers: Infinity War — $2,044,540,523
6) Jurassic World — $1,669,979,967
7) The Lion King (2019) — $1,654,367,425
8) Furious 7 — $1,516,881,526
9) The Avengers — $1,515,100,211
10) Frozen II — $1,445,182,280

This list says what has sold, and, according to theory, what will continue to sell tomorrow. And according to the list, that will, except for AVATAR and TITANIC, be a succession of sequels and remakes. This is a sobering thought. Especially to the executive. Even if she loves movies, even if she wants to do something original, this list must be lurking around somewhere in her mind. *It is what the people want.* Ostensibly.

Second, the trailer producer must understand the finished film. What influences it? Because it is a movie, and it was made by a filmmaker, by theory, the trailer producer can safely assume that other movies are influencing the finished film. But what of other movies? What were their appeals? How were they sold? How did they do it?

Third, the trailer producer must have a deep understanding of the audience. It is easy to find what they want, as one only has to again consult the list of the ten highest grossing films of all time. Why did audiences award these films with the highest grosses of all time? According to the list, they want sequels and remakes. Another STAR WARS, another JURASSIC PARK, another LION KING, another FAST AND FURIOUS. They want, alas, more of what worked yesterday. But what was that? What was the appeal? What *did* work yesterday so well that people are turning back to it today?

For that answer, it would be best to consult the same list—but this time adjusted for *inflation*.

1) Gone with the Wind — $3,739,000,000
2) Avatar — $3,286,000,000
3) Titanic — $3,108,000,000
4) Star Wars — $3,071,000,000
5) Avengers: Endgame — $2,823,000,000
6) The Sound of Music — $2,572,000,000
7) E.T. the Extra-Terrestrial — $2,511,000,000
8) The Ten Commandments — $2,377,000,000
9) Doctor Zhivago — $2,253,000,000
10) Star Wars: The Force Awakens — $2,221,000,000

This list reflects a more accurate representation of what the moviegoing public actually wants. At least, it reflects, a little better, overall tastes—past and present. Of course, it does not account for the changing landscape of media (people had less competing for their attention when GONE WITH THE WIND dominated theaters). But it does begin to indicate an interest in something beyond just aliens, sequels, and remakes. It shows that these are the films that endured; these are the films the viewing public, over a century of film-going, wanted. If the list reveals anything, it is that the audience does not just want sequels and remakes of past hits. To the contrary, the list shows, for the most part, a hunger for original programming.

But what of original programming? What, still, is the appeal of GONE WITH THE WIND? DOCTOR ZHIVAGO? What, still, was the appeal of E.T.? At least so much so that audiences ran out and spent billions of dollars watching them? What about STAR WARS, one of the most successful films of all time? Again, and again, the same question is asked, "What was the appeal?" If the trailer maker's job is to give the people what they want, then she must first understand what it is that the people want. She must understand what "the appeal" is.

Digging deeper, one could argue that this list reflects crass marketing appeal. The list represents films that were advertised to death. Ushered along by major corporations, these are the films whose studios paid for their attraction, ostensibly. Certainly, that case could be made for AVENGERS: END GAME; even more so for STAR WARS: THE FORCE AWAKENS; they are both sequels in firmly established film franchises, carrying high stakes that necessitated bundles of marketing dollars. Indeed, one could argue that these two films had a *built-in appeal*. They were going to be successful—regardless.

So, perhaps another list is worth considering. That of the 6th highest grossing weekend totals. It shows what hung around, five weeks after the initial hype left. This list, unlike the first two lists, reveals what endured after the marketing apparatus were slightly relieved. The following list shows *weekend* grosses, not overall.

1) American Sniper — $64,628,304
2) Avatar — $42,785,612
3) Titanic — $30,010,633
4) Gran Torino — $29,484,388
5) The Sixth Sense — $29,271,146
6) Black Panther — $26,650,690
7) Star Wars Ep. VII: The Force Awakens — $26,342,117
8) Paranormal Activity — $21,104,070
9) The Avengers — $20,486,418
10) Frozen — $19,642,107

This list reveals what had staying-power, absent any aggressive marketing, absent—for the most part—aliens. This list shows films that, in industry jargon, "had legs." They netted, for whatever reason, vast word of mouth. They resonated.

However, one could still argue that the public was feeling the after-effects of a massive advertising campaign—the trailers were still being shown, the posters still being promoted, at least, some-where. With that, one moves to a different list. That of what grossed the highest, in its *33rd weekend*. The following are weekend totals.

1) My Big Fat Greek Wedding — $5,854,005
2) Forrest Gump — $3,044,280
3) Raiders of the Lost Ark — $1,788,556
4) Chariots of Fire — $1,751,755
5) E.T. the Extra-Terrestrial — $1,368,496
6) The Sixth Sense — $1,280,780
7) Saving Private Ryan — $1,177,743
8) Titanic — $1,168,551
9) The Lion King — $1,108,308
10) Arthur — $933,000

This is a bewildering list, and completely incongruent with the top ten highest grossing films of all time—adjusted or not. Indeed, nothing on the list is a sequel, nothing on the list is a remake. The films are original and came, seemingly, out of nowhere. They also had transcended enough time to defy aspersions of having been marketed to their position. If any list is worth looking at to get a sense of what it is the public wants, to get a sense for how to make the correct appeal, this is the list to look to. It is, after all, what the public wanted. The list reflects what some group of people, at some point in time, independently wanted (independent of some corpo-ration marketing to them). Not just aliens, not just ghosts, not just explosions. At 33 weeks in, people were still seeking these films out, and therefore, by definition, these films, their grosses, tell us more about what people, in the long run, were and are looking for. Content not marked by just aliens or ghosts, but content marked by all sorts of subjects. Indeed, the sporadic sorts of subject bellies a confusion about what kind of content is of the most interest.

The executive looking at the list, the filmmaker looking at the list, the trailer producer, then asks what these films have in common. What does THE SIXTH SENSE share with SAVING PRIVATE RYAN? What does TITANIC hold with E.T.? What unites any of those films on the list? Not all had special effects. Very few in fact. Not all were 'period' pieces—THE SIXTH SENSE and MY BIG FAT GREEK WEDDING are set in the present. Certainly not all were sequels or remakes. ARTHUR, after all, is a picture about a drunk who sobers up and finds love; his story came out of nowhere. Not all are fantasy—SAVING PRIVATE RYAN and TITANIC are based on real events; FORREST GUMP takes its cues from reality, even if the central character is fictional. Indeed, few commonalities are found within any of these films.

Not even the old fallback of movie stars selling tickets can be assumed. How does one explain E.T., a film that went out of its way to be without stars (it famously cut out a scene with Harrison Ford)? Or for that matter, MY BIG FAT GREEK WEDDING, AVATAR, CHARIOTS OF FIRE, THE LION KING, and most of the films on that list? Tom Hanks was in the nascent stages of his star power with FORREST GUMP. Leonardo DiCaprio was still an unknown in TITANIC. Only THE SIXTH SENSE, SAVING PRIVATE RYAN, and RAIDERS OF THE LOST ARK could potentially be explained by their star power. And when one does look at the campaigns of those films, the stars were not heavily utilized.

The films in the list are clearly not unified by "star power."

What then remains?

What is the appeal of these films?

It is simply this: they are all classically designed. Which Robert McKee defines as, "a story built around an active protagonist who struggles against primarily external forces of antagonism to pursue his or her desire, through continuous time, within a consistent and causally connected fictional reality, to a closed ending of absolute, irreversible change" (McKee 1997, 45). Simply, a classically designed story is about a character or characters against the world, any world—so long as it's consistent—told to a resolute finish. Cole must help the ghosts who haunt him in THE SIXTH SENSE. Elliot must find a way to get E.T home. Jack and Rose must escape the sinking ship in TITANIC, or else. ARTHUR wins the affections of the girl, despite their class differences. The platoon in SAVING PRIVATE RYAN must navigate a war-torn Europe, fighting off the encroaching Nazis. And FORREST GUMP, despite the prejudices against his handicaps, blissfully puzzles through a 20th century landscape, influencing and changing history. The films on the list, indeed *any list* of financially successful films, are told through classical design.

Classical Storytelling Sells

Stories fall into a triumvirate, a triangle: classical design, minimalism, anti-plot (McKee 1997, 43). Classical design reigns at the top of the pyramid. Minimalism lives near the bottom, characterized by single or multiple characters, passively struggling, always at odds with their respective inner selves. In minimalism, the character is her own worst enemy. Examples are LOST IN TRANSLATION, THE ACCIDENTAL TOURIST, and RAGING BULL.

Anti-plots also live at the bottom of the triangle, but are further hemmed toward the right corner, typified by characters who struggle through inconsistent realities and time, whose struggles are completely internal, who ultimately find little or no resolution to their conflicts. Examples are 8 ½, INLAND EMPIRE, MULHOLLAND DRIVE. These films do not carry a universal appeal. Not through any lack of quality, but simply because of their natural addresses on the story triangle. As a rule, the further the film drifts from the classical to the minimal, to the anti-plot, the further the audience shrinks (McKee 1997, 62). Audiences are most attracted to the classical; least attracted to the anti-plot. If a century of box office is any indicator, then audiences are generally drawn to stories about heroes fighting outside foes. The audience, typically, and, as a safe bet, always wants their conflict outside of themselves, presented through consistent reality, time, and wrapped up with a definitive ending. It is what they believe to be the conflict of their own lives. Them against the world, in real time, in reality. Not themselves against themselves, scattered through a dreamworld that offers no end—à la LOST HIGHWAY, a quality film that did not sell at the box office.

This triumvirate, this triangle of story designs, defines where a story lives, of how well it will do with mass audiences. The highest grossing films—adjusted or not—all reflect works of classical storytelling. It's here where the trailer producer, aiming to give the audience what they want, must live and work. In classical storytelling, with characters struggling against outside forces, through consistent worlds and time, ultimately finding irreversible change. This is the ultimate appeal of all financially successful films.

It is classical story that unifies the commerce of popular film.

It is what the trailer producer must centralize her efforts around. Classical story. Not the selling of movie stars or special effects. Not the whims of an executive or the limitations of any given film. Classical story. It must be the trailer producer's first and foremost concern. The trailer producer is not in the business of selling motion pictures; she is instead in the business of selling classical stories that come in the form of motion pictures.

It is that which this book is concerned with.

Selling film through story.

2

SELLING STORY

It's one thing to tell story in the scope of a 400-page novel. It's another to relay it in the duration of two hours. It is another entirely, when compressed down to the short film, to tell it in thirty minutes or less. The difficulty increases geometrically when the story is reduced to two minutes. Much is compressed, much is lost. And must be so for the purpose of *selling*. Of course, this opens the door for mystery, for intrigue—and a dearth of information, a scarcity of content by nature imbues in the viewer a want to know more. But it is easy to compress to the point of bewilderment, confusion; trailer making can't be a matter of chopping bits into a stew and seeing what comes up. The result of that is "montage," a collection of images strung together with no coherent purpose other than to highlight that a film has been made and that it includes pictures of various artifacts. It is important to realize that a trailer is more than just a montage of video clips and music. Montage has its place—but that comes later. The trailer producer must first design a structure that ultimately places expectations of some sort into the audience's mind and be able to ignite those expectations into desire to pay good money to see that film. It must sell story.

This sounds like an overwhelming, unworkable task. Especially when it is such a vague dictum to begin with. What does it mean to sell "story?"

One could break down the elements of story. Character, scene, sequence, act, resolution—the makeup of narrative. Character is concerned with the people who make up the movie, someone—or some group of someones—striving for a goal. The *characters*. A scene is a vignette of time and space whereupon a character sets out to accomplish one goal of value change and ends up with another—possibly one that is deeper, wider in scope than the previous. A sequence is a collection of scenes. An act is a collection of sequences that culminate around a larger value change in the character's life—boy meets girl, boy loses girl, building blows up, bad guy gets away, bad guy is captured, bad guy is killed, etc., et all. These changes further deepen the scope of the character's quest, goals, agency, and purpose. Resolution means, simply, the story comes to an end.

But what does any of that even mean? How is understanding the nature of scene to help in constructing a trailer? What is it to say that a trailer should be made up of "three acts?" On its own, the information is meaningless; a collection of empty rhetorical devices, tools which have no purpose. It is important instead to *present* these rhetorical effects of story, to express them, in minutes, and do so in an appealing manner. "Appealing" meaning one that's captivating; "captivating" meaning one that raises the audience's interest and creates a demand in them to know more; demand meaning a movement—or determined movement—to buy tickets, video-on-demands, DVDs, Blu-rays, etc. A "want" to see the picture. A "desire" to find out "what happens."

No small task.

This ordeal explodes when confronted with the movie itself. If anything will conjure an overwhelming dread, what the artist refers to as "the blank canvas," it will be the movie itself. There is just too much material, too much stimuli. The film's images and sound create a multi-faceted effect that is debilitating, paralyzing. The trailer producer is still asking "what about this am I supposed to sell?"

Where To Find Story

The first step is to sever the connection between image and sound. The trailer producer, editor, the team involved, then—and this is important—***turns off the images.*** In the beginning stages of selling a film's story, the images are the least important and the most likely to confuse and distract from what is most important: the dialogue. Not the music, not the sound effects, and certainly not the images. These are all secondary elements to be dealt with later. It is the dialogue that is most paramount. It is imperative, if only for this reason, that the three aspects of a film's audio—the music, sound effects, and dialogue—all be on separate, individual tracks. No work can be done unless these elements are each isolated. It is all in the effort to isolate the film's dialogue.

Movies are often considered a visual medium, the visual championed over the sound. In reality, the order is flipped. It is the sound that motivates a motion picture. Not the pictures. If the trailer editor started with the images, cutting in the picture, the best "trailer worthy" shots, he would then have to go back and find dialogue, or some kind of voiceover to support the claims made by the images. That is an almost impossible task. Because the truth is, most films are not first constructed out of their images—they are first *written*, through a script, through dialogue. For most writers, it is through their dialogue that they are telling a story. And it is story that the trailer producer must be most concerned with.

Therefore, a trailer editor will find his story in the film's dialogue. This is what it means to show, and not tell.

Types of Dialogue

To begin creating a trailer, the editor must go through the movie and extract the relevant dialogue, then assemble that dialogue—without pictures—into a coherent and compelling whole. Of course, this begs the question: what kind of dialogue should the trailer editor be on the lookout for? All dialogue? No. There are just too many hems and haws, too many "hey, how ya' doins'?" to work through in a typical film. The trailer editor must be on watch for very specific types of dialogue.

There are only two: exposition and action. Exposition is *where someone is giving information about the world of the story*. Action is *where someone is trying to get something with their words*.

First, exposition. This is information that is needed to follow the world of the story. Robert McKee defines it as: "facts—the information about setting, biography, and characterization that the audience needs to know to follow and comprehend the events of the story" (McKee 1997, 334). It is material about the world of the story, the character's background, their history. It comes from anyone stating any kind of fact about the world of their tale. Some examples of expositional dialogue include:

- "You've been here for 6 months."
- "The enemy forces are closing in."
- "You haven't been looking too well."

A perfect example of excellent exposition—and therefore trailer worthy dialogue—is in Gore Verbinski's horror film THE RING.

The one character asks her friend, "Have you heard about this videotape that kills you when you watch it?" She continues, "You start to play it and it's like somebody's nightmare." This explains almost everything you need to know about the film. Which is why the producers used it in the trailer. THE RING went on to open at number one, ultimately grossing $130 million dollars.

There is a reason why every trailer begins with some variation of "In a world where," or, "In a time when." They are both fundamental pieces of exposition—they are both facts about the story's setting. They explain the 'when' and 'where.' Further types of exposition could be the who, what, and why. Also, backstory in general. Especially anytime anyone says anything about a character like, "You've been here for six months."

Exposition, information about the world of the film's story, is one type of dialogue the trailer editor looks for.

The second type of dialogue is action. This is the characters using their words to get something they want. Action-oriented dialogue could range from something as simple as, "Give me the detonator!" to… "I love looking in your eyes." The latter being a little more about inference, the former being more direct. In the first trailer for DUNKIRK, a captain tries to motivate his mate into war, "There's no hiding from this, son. We have a job to do." The mate refuses, "If we go there, we'll die." Action-oriented dialogue bellies a subtext; here, it is the mate's desire to stay far away from Dunkirk. In a good movie, no one really should be talking unless they're trying to "get" something—whether it's a million dollars, or something more abstract like love, or attention. "We need to get to the ship now!" is action-dialogue because it is the speaker attempting to motivate everyone off the ship immediately. Contrast that with "The ship is designed to carry passengers through water." Which is only stating a fact about the ship in question. Action-dialogue is always characterized by someone trying to get what they want.

In making a trailer, it is all about the arrangement of dialogue. An understanding of its nature is imperative.

To really understand dialogue, and its various uses, shades, mysteries, the trailer producer would do well to read Robert McKee's book, *Dialogue*. It is as comprehensive as any work about writing, especially writing dialogue. For the trailer editor looking to arrange movie-talk, it is a must read.

Arranging Dialogue

The trailer editor must go through the entire film, isolating any dialogue clips that fulfill the role of exposition and action. He must keep these two separate, as they will need to be drawn from respectively. Once the film has been thoroughly scoured, the editor then has to arrange the exposition to tell a story. He does this by alternating between exposition and action. First, he inserts a little exposition. Then, a little action. Then he builds on this, going back and forth, drawing on the principles of storytelling, adding and subtracting, arranging and re-arranging into scene, sequence, act, resolution, until all at once the trailer's structure reveals itself to him.

First, the trailer editor starts with some exposition. On the timeline, he places the audio clips that "set the story." This would mean first looking for the vaguest piece of exposition. Out of all the assembled clips, what in the exposition 'bin' is the vaguest—and says something about the world of the story? For example, the trailer for AVENGERS: INFINITY WAR begins with "The entire time I knew him, he only ever had one goal." The line raises questions about 'who' and 'why.' Raising questions is the purpose of vagueness. The trailer editor then needs to, as McKee says, "pace out the exposition." Putting the least important facts at the beginning of the trailer, the most important at the end.

Then the trailer editor puts in a little bit of action-oriented dialogue. In the trailer for JURASSIC WORLD, the mom gently tells her sons, "If something chases you: run." It too is vague in that it raises questions about who or what might eventually be chasing them. Early choices should be made based on how many questions the piece of dialogue raises.

As the trailer editor works through the trailer, he moves from the indistinct, the generic, to the more specific, the germane. In the JURASSIC WORLD trailer, the owner of the park says, "We have learned more in the past decade from genetics than a century of digging up bones." She continues, "We have our first, genetically modified hybrid." After enough interest about the new monsters have been established, about how powerful they are, after enough curiosity has been aroused, after a clear enough picture about the universe of JURASSIC WORLD has been developed, the Chris Pratt character simply says… "Evacuate the island."

In making a trailer, it is ALL about finding the right dialogue, then stringing that dialogue together in the correct sequence. That is, the audio clips go back and forth within an argumentative structure, one providing a problem, the other providing a solution—and vice versa.

In the trailer for DUNKIRK, a soldier shouts, "They need to send more ships!"

Another soldier responds, "They've activated the civilian boats."

The response? "Civilians!? We need destroyers!"

A solution, a problem.

"You're weekend sailors, not a bloody navy," a soldier rebukes. "You should be at home!"

"There's no hiding from this, son."

A problem, a solution. A question, an answer. A negative, a positive. That is the drama. On and on, building back and forth between opposites, between arguments, until the dialectic climaxes around a final solution:

"Turn it around!" the soldier finally screams.

When DUNKIRK was released, everyone already knew the ending. Like TITANIC, audiences showed not to see *what* would happen, but *to see how it would unfold.* In other words, the trailer editor built interest by *revealing* information, not concealing it. Through dialectics, through argument, through presentation of evidence from the film itself. Curiosity is piqued by reveal, not concealment. The audience wants information, not intrigue. The notion of film-spoilers is a hysteria of the internet-age. It is through revealed information that the viewer begins to build a mental model of the film, writing the movie in their own mind, needing to discover how it will all turn out. Robert Zemeckis (director of BACK TO THE FUTURE, CAST AWAY, and WHAT LIES BENEATH) puts it well: "The reason McDonald's is a tremendous success is that you don't have any surprises. You know exactly what it is going to taste like. Everybody knows the menu." People want to know what they are getting into. They want to see the movie before they see it—the whole purpose of watching a movie trailer.

It tells a story. It *sells* a story.

Take, for example, the trailer for THE MATRIX. It begins, "The Matrix is the wool that has been pulled over your eyes, to blind you from the truth." The hero, Neo, seeing the reality of the Matrix, can only scream, "Get me the hell out of here!"

When out of the Matrix, he is confronted with a single question: "So you're here to save the world?"

His answer? "[I need] guns, lots of guns."

The audience immediately projects a film about a one-man army waging war against everything and anything. Through the selection and arrangement of exposition and actions, the trailer editor curated a presentation of expectations, visions of what the actual film would be—in this case, one man taking on the world.

Imagination creates expectation, expectation causes curiosity, curiosity causes the viewer to imagine, imagination creates demand. As McKee says, "skillful marketing creates genre expectation" (McKee 1997, 90). **Movie success is all about the creation of expectations. Phenomenal movie success is about exceeding those expectations.** THE MATRIX skillfully marketed expectation, eventually opening to $28 million, ultimately surpassing viewer expectations, grossing over $400 million dollars, and creating demand for three more sequels.

It is the trailer producer's job to curate expectation, position it, and project it to the audience. What promises need to be made? What promises can be backed up? It is easy to lie in a movie trailer—and most movie trailers do that—and most trailers would be WISE to do that—but what is not so easy is to deal with not meeting those expectations. That is called "bad word of mouth." Which is created when the trailer explicitly promises one thing and delivers another. Consider the trailer for the 1995 film JURY DUTY. The trailer shows a slacker being summoned for jury duty; when he is on the steps of the courthouse, he looks offscreen and shouts, "There's OJ!" This implied that the movie was about the famous OJ Simpson murder case, itself a popular news item in real life at the time. Of course, the film is not about the OJ Simpson murder case; when audiences discovered this, they savaged JURY DUTY and the film died at the box office.

Contrast that with the trailer for INCEPTION, a blockbuster film supposedly about dream thieves.

The trailer starts off with the Cobb character introducing himself:

"There's one thing you should know about me."

"I specialize in a very specific type of security."

"Subconscious security."

Then, so as to not confuse the audience with the word "subconscious," the trailer supplies another character who says, "*You're talking about dreams."*

These four audio clips, taken from different parts of the film, have very little to do with one another. But juxtaposed, they create fertile expectation: an interest to understand the very complicated premise of INCEPTION.

"Mr. Cobb has a job offer he'd like to discuss with you," the one character says.

"Kind of a work placement?" The other character asks.

The audience feels they are being invited along on a journey.

"Not exactly," The Cobb character retorts.

Now the audience is thinking about dreams, about dream security, about a film that takes place inside the mind.

"We create the world of the dream," the main character explains.

"We bring the subject into that dream…."

"…And they fill it with their secrets."

Then the other character interrupts, "And you break in and steal it."

This is a film about dream thieves.

The Cobb character announces, "It's called Inception."

However, the process just outlined is *not* called Inception. It's actually, as explained in the film, called Extraction. Did it matter? The film stayed at number 1 for three consecutive weeks. Audiences showed up expecting a film about thieves stealing dreams and instead were given an even better one about thieves *planting* dreams. The plot is actually about a group of bandits who break into a young man's mind and *plant* the idea for him to create his own empire. The actual premise ended up being more interesting, more complex, than the promised one. The trailer producer's masterstroke was in 1) recognizing that the film's premise would have been too complicated and too far-fetched to explain in a trailer (why and how does someone plant dreams?), and 2) re-structuring the dialogue to create a comprehensive expectation. In other words, it was the trailer's job to warm up the audience—not just for anticipation, but for understanding. A trailer's top priority, other than to sell, is to create a position in the film goer's imagination; a position that can then ultimately be fulfilled, understood—and, in the case of INCEPTION—exceeded (the filmed grossed almost a billion dollars and was nominated for Best Picture). This is all done through the arrangement of the film's dialogue. It is up to the trailer editor to arrange the dialogue in such a way that the audience begins creating holes in their own psyche to receive information about the film, begin processing that information, and then create impressions about what is being promoted. It is important to remember Christian Metz's words that "Films release a mechanism of affective and perceptual participation in the spectator" (Metz, 1990, 4). Trailers are designed to stimulate, not sedate. To initiate, not placate. It is not about overselling or underselling, it is about managing expectations so that they may be fulfilled, and then, hopefully, exceeded.

A Method for Arranging Dialogue

It takes a lot of study to really, fully, grasp the best way of arranging dialogue. The trailer editor, concerned with getting better at this aspect of the craft, should find five other trailers similar to the movie he is working on. Then, with each trailer, he should turn off the video, or look away, and write down every line of dialogue on separate notecards. He then reviews the order of the notecards, taking note of the arrangement, really feeling it, really remembering it. If the trailer editor does this exercise enough, he will develop an almost sixth sense for how to properly arrange expositional and action-dialogue. In addition, he will find himself watching movies with a totally different set of eyes and ears—that of a true trailer editor and producer. When a character in a movie says something of expositional or action quality, of "trailer worth," it will just leap out. Which is how the trailer editor really knows he is getting good at his craft.

It is in the selection and arranging of dialogue where the foundation of trailer editing begins. The trailer editor must become an expert at this skill. From here, it is a matter of knowing which expectations to create, and how to best deliver on those expectations.

In the following chapter, the trailer editor will learn how to make rhythm out of his arrangement of dialogue.

3

A TRAILER'S RHYTHM

Which Comes First: Music or Sound?

Once the dialogue has been arranged, the producer is faced with two paths forward: she could work on the music first, or the sound first. Both choices influence the other. The trailer producer, tempted to get going, could find her way through with a series of haphazard guesses—she could find a bunch of trailer sound effects and start dropping them in the timeline. Or, tempted even further still, she could seek out an appropriate piece of music—appropriate to the material at hand—and begin building from there. She could use the music to "edit against." But what if there is no music? Or worse still, what if there is music—but no clearance to use that song? It is often one of the first disillusionments of any producer or editor to find out that music is copyrighted and cannot be used indiscriminately. It costs tens of thousands of dollars, perhaps hundreds of thousands, in some cases millions, to use a particular song legally, unfettered of any future interference. Many trailers have been edited to, designed with, a very specific song; it's only later that the producer discovers the song, no matter how great, can't be used.

Or, worse still: the trailer is finished, sent out, and then later scrubbed from the market due to a cease-and-desist letter from the song's publisher. Music is that important. A team of lawyers could shut down an entire, well-made trailer, based solely on the music itself.

What's worse is that music, in large part, determines a trailer's underlying flow. It determines the entire structure. Imagine building a house without first the basement, the foundation. Imagine having to build the upper floors on…nothing. But what is the trailer editor supposed to do? What is she supposed to "edit" to? How is she supposed to go about doing any kind of work? Simply, what is anyone at this stage supposed to do, given all the challenges?

The Problem Redefined

First, all these questions must be put out of mind. A clean slate is needed.

Second, the entire problem has to be redefined to that of finding a trailer's main rhythm. In other words, finding its correct BPM. What is BPM? It stands for beats per minute. It is how a heart rate is measured. For instance, a normal heart rests between 60 and 100 beats per minute. This is a calm, routine range. Anything over 100 beats is approaching fast. Anything under 60, bradycardia sets in—a serious problem.

It is a heart's tempo.

If beats per minute is the rhythm of a human heartbeat, then tempo is the relative fast or slowness of its speed (Hewitt 2008, 40). It is how slow or fast the music is moving. The song Mombasa, created by Hans Zimmer for a fast chase scene in the movie INCEP-TION, is 144 beats per minute. For the trailer producer, it is a matter of how fast or slow the trailer moves. Beats per minute defines a trailer's tempo. Less than 60 beats per minute would be too slow. More than 180—too fast. But that is the range: 60-180 beats per minute. At least, that is the range for a typical trailer. A drama, for instance, would have an average tempo of 75 beats per minute—although it could be faster. An action film, for instance would have an average tempo of 140 beats per minute—although, it too could be slower. It depends on what speed and scope the trailer producer and editor are aiming for. Is the trailer fast and quick? Then a 120 BPM and over would be good. Is the trailer slow, but intense? A beats per minute between 60 and 75 might be accurate.

Hans Zimmer, in his Masterclass, refers to beats per minute as the spacing on lined composition paper. It is the guiding force for his compositions. In contrast, beats per minute are the lined composition paper for trailer production. It is what, in effect, is edited against, and guides the tempo and rhythm of the trailer. Therefore, a trailer's beats per minute must, first and foremost, be discovered by the trailer producer. This is done by a tool called the "metronome." The Merriam Webster's Collegiate Dictionary refers to "metronome" as "an instrument designed to mark exact time by a regularly repeated tick." The word is derived from the Ancient Greek of némo, meaning, "I manage," "I lead." A metronome is the device sitting atop the piano that clicks back and forth.

This device can be acquired in a few forms. One, as a plain old metronome that sits above a piano and clicks back and forth. This is the exact device the Morgan Freeman character used to soothe himself to sleep in the film SEVEN. Two, a metronome device can be found on the computer, which is preferable, as the sounds of the clicks and the dings can be customized to the user's preference. Even better still is for the trailer producer to download a metronome "app" for her cell phone, so she can go on long walks, listening to just the sound, varying in the different beats per minute, subconsciously garnering an understanding of what it means to hear tempo. The device can also be found in any digital audio workstation like Logic X or Abelton, usually at the top of the interface, as it's the most important aspect of any music creation program.

It is first crucial to understand what these various clicks and dings are demarcating. Simply, they are describing a single metric cycle—a single measure—a single bar. As Michael Hewitt writes, "[a bar is] a term which arose from the practice of drawing a vertical line on the score after the completion of each metric cycle." A bar determines each metric cycle. With a metronome, that would sound like, "ding, click, click, click....ding, click, click, click." Each ding represents the beginning of a new bar, a new metric cycle.

Time Signatures

Each metric cycle is determined by a time signature. Simply, how many beats within that bar? Most music contains 4 beats per bar; that is, 4/4 time. 4 beats per bar, each beat is a quarter. It is important for the trailer producer to know that most, if not all, trailers are playing in 4/4 time. That is, again to reiterate, 4 beats each bar, done so with each beat taking up a quarter of that bar. Of course, there are other time signatures. 5/4, is another example. This one saying that five beats will occur within one bar of music—either with 3 beats and a quick 2 to round off the bar, or with 2 beats and 3 to round off the bar. The measure is designed to be irregular and create a sense that something is not right. This is, not coincidently, the time signature for the theme song to John Carpenter's HALLOWEEN. It plays in 5/4 time, creating an uneven rhythm that is designed to underscore the evil of the Michael Myers character. Two other unusual time signatures, used less often, are 6/8 and 7/8. These two are used when a "rushed" feeling is warranted. They can make a trailer feel frantic, or "off-kilter."

With an understanding of time signature, the trailer producer can then determine the correct tempo of her work. There are two ways to do this. One, by instinct alone. The trailer producer dials about the tempo, first slow, then fast, finding which neighborhood the trailer—or a part of the trailer—should be in. Two, the trailer editor arranges the dialogue, and then uses the speed of the dialogue's arrangement to decipher tempo. Each line of dialogue is placed right before the first beat, just as the current metric cycle is about to end. This is the more likely choice, as it corresponds with the exact underlying nature of what the trailer wants; the speed of the actor's talking, the natural pauses between each, the duration of those pauses, will all point to a certain beats per minute. The trailer producer should not be surprised what tempo the trailer is dictating. One might think a trailer should start off slow; but then, the trailer tells her, in fact, that a faster range, more like 120 BPM, would be apt. It is ultimately whatever feels right.

Royalty Free Music

Beyond having nothing to work with, sometimes the trailer producer can obtain what is called "royalty free" music. This is music without legal clearances placed on it; music that can be used in the final trailer, free of any royalty payments to the original music composer, or original publishing house; the kind of music most trailer editors reach for, as usually no one involved in the project can afford to pay a "royalty" fee for every time the trailer (playing the music) is played. Provided the trailer producer has such music—what then? Does the trailer producer just layer in the music, then have the editor begin cutting away to it? Perhaps.

Invisible Music

But another option is available. The song—whether it is royalty free or not—is placed into a digital audio workstation like Logic Pro X. The producer applies a "beats per minute counter." Other workstations have a similar tool, but for here, we will stay with Logic Pro. This tool analyzes the beats per minute simply by "listening" to the song; a number will eventually flash—this is the beats per minute of the song, the song's tempo. The editor writes this number down, then adjusts what is called the program's master clock—another way of saying 'tempo'—to match the song's beats per minute. Then, the editor prints out, renders out, a scratch of silence—say, two minutes—but with the program's metronome turned on. This can be done whether music is available or not. This, in effect, exports a two-minute sound of the metronome playing at that exact tempo.

Once the editor places the sound file in the video editing program, the file will reflect the exact waveform of whatever tempo has been selected. The waveform will demonstrate where each beat occurs. The waveform won't show a bout of spikes flying everywhere, as would be the case with an actual song.

The waveform of a file showing its beats per minute. This "beat" is easy to edit to.

This is what the editor edits to. An exact visual representation of a metronome lining out the selected tempo.

Because not only will this sound file's waveform show where the beats are occurring, it will display, if programmed correctly, where the metric cycle ends and begins, where the new bar starts. It is within, or rather, above, this bar where the editor will place his clips of dialogue. It is by locating these clips in each subsequent bar that will render the trailer's actual rhythm, as dictated by the metronome—a core representation of time's passage.

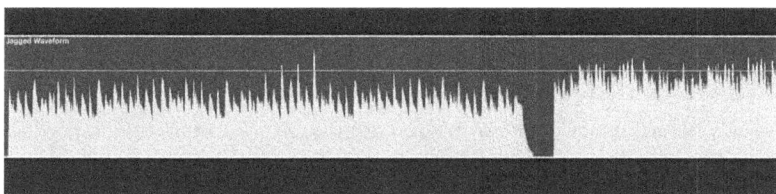

A jagged waveform. Not easy to edit to.

It is for this reason that the editor must understand that time in video editing is not the same as real time. In video editing, time itself is not to be trusted. A second can feel like a minute. A split second can feel like ten seconds. It is, as Einstein says about time, very relative. Which, here, is relative to the subjective state of the viewer. A simple measuring of timecode cannot be used alone. It is the beats per minute, the tempo of an invisible song, that provides the actual timing of a trailer's pace.

The trailer producer and editor, whether they are the same person or not, must shape the trailer to some kind of tempo. This is usually the tempo set by the dialogue. An actual tempo then, shaped by, as Scott Billups says, "a thousand years of refinement," is required to fill out the spaces between the dialogue. Each metric cycle is what provides the holding cells, the holding patterns, for the dialogue; the ending of those metric cycles—or rather, the beginning of the next metric cycle, is exactly where a trailer's major impacts will go.

This takes out all the guess work of "editing to the beat." This shows where the beat actually is, and where exactly its corresponding material must go. It is within the metronome, the "click track," where the true tempo and rhythm of a trailer will be found—regardless of if the trailer producer and editor have their song or not.

It is up to the trailer producer, editor, sound engineer, the team—or the sole operator—to determine the order of musical operations for each individual trailer. Some trailer-making situations come with music in hand—the trailer editor can simply assess the beats-per-minute then go right to the editing stage. This is a rare situation due to music usually being copyrighted. Usually, a song has to be located, cleared, and negotiated. Or, at the very least, it must be *found*. Then it must be compared against *other* songs, tested against the material, weighed, and then selected. Indeed, sometimes a song needs to be swapped out for another. To say that music-choosing is a nerve-wracking process is an understatement. It can be seen as the structure of the trailer itself, and therefore the very lifeblood of everything that will be done.

No Music, No Problem

What about if the trailer producer doesn't have any access to royalty free music? Which is usually the case (royalty free doesn't always mean "worldwide use," which is what is actually needed). What if the producer does not have *any* music? The production has supplied her an absolute drought of musical material—the soundtrack isn't any good, or it doesn't lend itself to the hype of a trailer soundtrack, or the rights are tied up in some odd legal matter.

What then?

A trailer producer can enact several strategies.

For one, she can fill up the soundtrack of the trailer-to-be with *just sound effects.* In which case, music then is not needed, and the producer can go ahead searching through her personal vault of sound effects. But that is usually not enough. Even sound-designed trailers require a great deal of musical undertone—or at the least, a great deal of musical structuring.

For another, a trailer producer can resign herself to hiring a composer. There are any number of composers out in the field who work at composing music specifically for movie trailers. These individuals, while out there, are rare, and are usually working for record labels who will exact a hefty fee for not only the production of a song, but of its ultimate rights and fee structure. This is not an ideal situation for the usual trailer producer. Especially the independent trailer producer. There is usually no budget for such a matter. Nevertheless, if a composer was to be hired, the trailer editor would go ahead with arranging the film's dialogue, and then edit to a bare click track, dropping in shots to correspond with the various ticks on the soundtrack; the production would then be shuttled over to the composer who would apply the music based on the clicks (the composer would be very appreciative of there having already been an established beats per minute assigned to the piece); eventually, the trailer and music accompanying would come back, and that would be that.

But for most trailer productions, this is not a realistic aspiration.

So, ultimately, one is left with the only inevitable conclusion: the music must be made in-house.

This is a terrifying proposition for most producers and editors in the video/film field. Their training has only ever prepared them to deal with the visual realm—and, within a limited scope—sound. The act of composing music has always been left to the composer, the music producer. Composing music comes as bad news to the classically trained trailer producer and video editor.

Thankfully, there are shortcuts. One of them begins with letting go of pre-conceived notions. The trailer producer needs to relieve her mind of what music was once "envisioned"—to use a visual term—and allow for whatever it is she can cook up in the laboratory. She will be surprised to learn that most trailer music is, in fact, incidental. That is to say, the makers of a trailer, if guided to the end, will discover that the music doesn't really matter. That is also to say, much of the music will be smothered beneath dialogue—or, at least, it can be smothered beneath much of the dialogue. The music will be hemmed in by a great deal of the sound effects (of which the trailer-editor will be less worried about utilizing). The music, to everyone's surprise, will ultimately not matter. Or, at least, it can be positioned to not matter. The trailer can be produced to favor sound effects over music.

Another shortcut is in having a basic understanding of music theory. This is a scary proposal. But in reality, it should not be. The production team, the editor, the producer, need to understand that music theory, like the film education they've so assiduously acquired, can be, at least, grasped, if not overcome, if not, ultimately, and with repeated attempts, mastered.

Music production can be done.

Of course, that word "production" bodes the fact that not only must the music be created, but it must also be *produced*. That is to say, music must be written—if not composed, designed—and then brought to life with instruments. The process can be grasped, and, eventually, can become a familiar face. Music *production*—again, the use of instruments, mixing—dovetails very much into the world of sound design. It is about keeping an open mind to this and not being afraid of the foreign grounds of music as a field.

Learning A New Language

Is it necessary to start from scratch with music theory? Will this become a tome on music education, rather than an instruction on creating movie trailers? Yes and no. First, music has to be seen as another means of communication—*not as a means of co-opting another field entirely.* It goes without saying that a thorough understanding of music must be garnered by anyone in the film field; the more in-depth, the better. It goes without saying because film, video, whatever visual medium is being used, is music. That is to say, the visual, what the audience sees, is heavily dependent upon the underlying soundtrack. It is not a stretch to add that trailers, at the end of the day, are music videos. It is no coincidence that the vast majority of the great directors were also, at one time in their careers, music video directors. Martin Scorsese, for example.

Music is film. Film is music.

It is one of the great misfortunes of film education that music theory, music production, isn't seen as a foregone conclusion to a well-grounded understanding of the field itself.

However, reality comes into question. How realistic is it, in the span of this instruction, to impart the entire field of music education? How far can the reader stray from matters of video editing and sound selection to learn about the outer reaches of extended chords, of advanced harmony, of music mastering? Of course, it is not very realistic. Nor is it fair to suddenly ask of a video editor, trailer producer, to know, let alone master, let alone imbue themselves with the spirit of music. Just as some people are not pro athletes, some people, most artists, are not professional musicians. There has to be an accounting for that intangible quality called talent. There also has to be an accounting for time, which is always in short supply. No one involved in the creation of a trailer (nor anyone reading this instruction) can just absorb the foundations of music theory and production.

To the relief of the reader, the fundamentals can be re-arranged. To anyone in need of fast music—and fairly good music—and in need of instruction for such items—the teaching of music theory and production can be greatly re-arranged and therefore compressed. It can be presented so that the trailer producer will ultimately have a Swiss-Army knife of knowledge to approach music with. She will not be Hans Zimmer. But she will have the tools, and the insights, to improvise a tune.

A trailer producer *can* also be a music producer.

The following is how.

4

MUSIC DESIGN

As a note: *The trailer producer must exercise extreme patience with the following material. While greatly compressed, it is still technical; it requires not only a close read, but a closer re-read. It is best to take the material slowly.*

Home Base

First, the trailer producer has to know the keys, the notes. He must know which ones are which. 'A', 'B', 'C', 'D', 'E', 'F', 'G'.

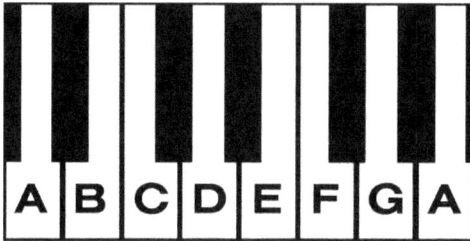

It is important to know which keys are which. Thankfully, there are only 7 important ones.

These keys, these notes, and only these, will be his home. He must know that these notes are always played in some kind of scale. What is a scale? A scale is a palette of notes that, when played together, will sound nice. They will sound *in harmony.*

Scale is all about keeping harmony. It is all about staying in *key.*

For the trailer producer, it is about keeping the music sounding cohesive. And for all intents and purposes, it would serve the trailer producer to just stay in scale.

Counting Steps

Each note is made up of a "half-step." This includes the black keys. When the trailer producer counts the keys on a piano, he must realize he is actually counting steps. It is important to re-iterate that. Counting keys is counting "steps." Each gap between each key represents a *step.* So, one key up to a black key: that's a *half step.* The black key down to a white key? That's *another half step.*

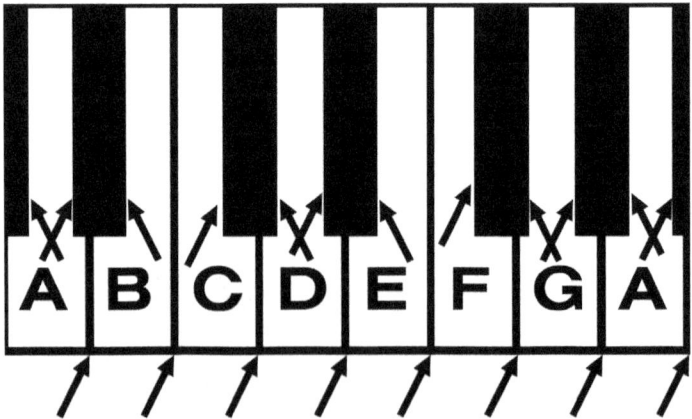

The arrows all point to half-steps.

What does a step represent? A step represents a "semitone." Think of it like this: going to the right on a piano is rising a step. The producer would be wise to plink each key on a piano and note how with each "step," each key, the sound moves "up" in pitch. Then, the producer should move to the left, noting how with each "step," each key, the sound moves "down" in pitch.

That is a semi-tone. Notches on a line of pitch.

That is what a keyboard is. A series of pitches.

The 'A' key represents one pitch. The 'B' a slightly higher. The 'C', even higher still. And so on, right along the keyboard.

Of course, this does not consider the black keys.

What are they?

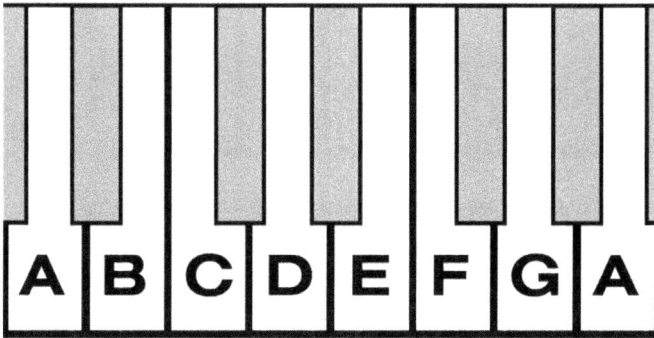

The black keys, here shaded gray, represent a semi-tone.

They are simply a half-step "up" or "down" in pitch from the white key. Called either a flat or a sharp, depending on what scale the musician is in, these keys serve to provide a half of a semi-tone between each white key. In other words, if one wanted to move up a "semi-tone," a "half-step," then one would just move from the white key up to the black key. That is a "half-step." That is a "semi-tone." Nothing more, nothing less.

Important Notes & The Octave

Next, it is important to know that a keyboard only—really—has 12 notes on it. 'A' through 'G'. These notes then simply go right up and down the keyboard. 'A', 'B', 'C', 'D', 'E', 'F', 'G'—then, again—'A', 'B', 'C', 'D', 'E', 'F', 'G'.

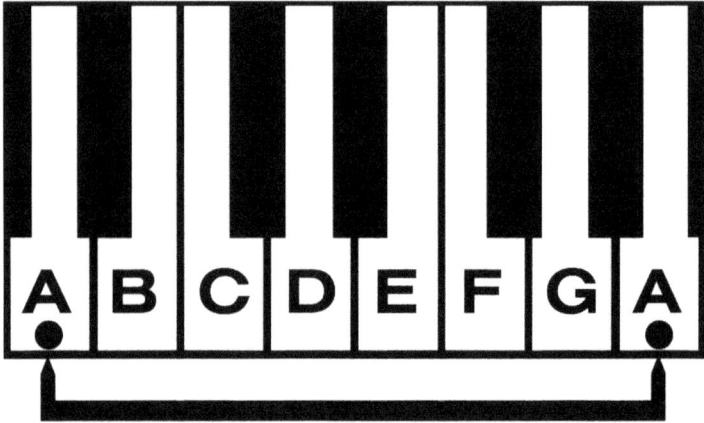

An octave runs right through the first letters
of the alphabet, then stops.

Why it does not continue with the rest of the alphabet is a matter of pitch. After the 'G' note (or, technically, the 'G' sharp note), an OCTAVE is reached. 'A', 'B', 'C', 'D', 'E', 'F', 'G' makes up an entire octave. An octave is the distance between one note, and its similarly named note found either to the right, or to the left in pitch. An octave is also the distance between one musical pitch. So, in other words, if the musician liked a note, but wanted a deeper note, he would move to the "left," and find the similarly named note. That note would be the same note, but deeper.

It has a deeper pitch.

That is as much understanding as a trailer editor need know about octaves.

Perhaps it would also be good to note that doubling up octaves—playing the same note in different octaves—creates a rich, deep sound. Playing them in fast succession creates an interesting pulse.

But finding out those special effects is a matter of trial-and-error.

It is simply important to note the octave and know that the keyboard is only made up of 12 "notes." 'A', 'B', 'C', 'D', 'E', 'F', 'G'. Knowing this eliminates a great deal of apprehension and mystery about what all the other notes on a keyboard are. It also lets the trailer producer know what is germane to his knowledge of music.

Scales

To get a real, tactile feel of these notes, the trailer producer should practice what is called the 'C' scale. That is, the trailer producer should place all five hands on the keyboard—the thumb on the 'C' key, index on the 'D', middle on the 'E', then, play 'C', 'D', 'E'. Just before hitting the 'F' key, he should press down harder on the 'E' key, then tuck his thumb under, and then user his thumb to hit the 'F' key; then play the rest of the notes up to the 'C' with the rest of the fingers. Then, once reaching 'C' with the pinky finger, hit the same note again, and reverse the process. The trailer producer, the make-shift musician, should do this many, many times. The practice is called "scales." Doing so will imbue each note into the subconscious of the listener/player, who will ultimately come to do it faster and faster, ultimately garnering a sense of… playing the piano!

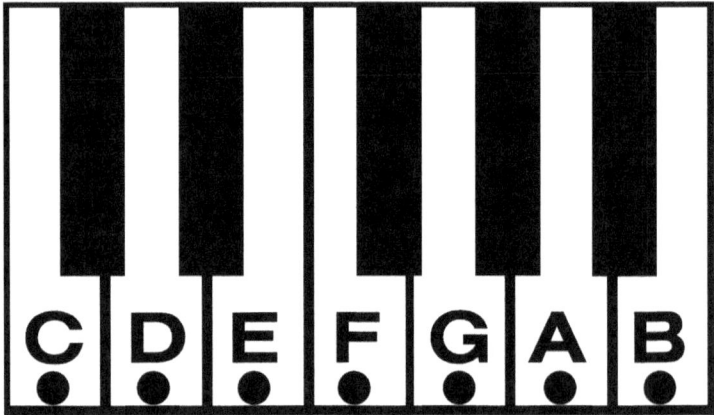

The C Major scale.

That's it.

Or, at least, that's it for playing what is called 'C' major. The most basic of all scales.

Unfortunately, 'C' major is not what most dramatic music is played in (although, it can be quite dramatic nonetheless; don't be quick to discount it).

What is important here is to learn that for every major scale, there is a corresponding MINOR scale. And the minor scale is what is most important for making dramatic, brooding tense, music. How does the minor go? More importantly, and in line with the previous example, how does 'C' minor go?

It is… 'C', 'D'—then, the producer should move up a half pitch to the black key on the right. This will be 'D' sharp. Then, he SKIPS over 'E', lands on 'F'. Pushes 'G'. THEN, moves up a half-pitch, a half-step to its corresponding black key on the right. This is 'G' sharp. Then—and this is the tricky part—he skips over 'A', and instead pushes the black key that is just to the right of 'A'. This is 'A' sharp. Then, he skips over 'B', and lands on 'C'.

The C Minor scale.

This is 'C' minor. The producer should play this repeatedly; then play 'C' major repeatedly. The producer should note the difference between the two "sounds." It is the difference between a major and a minor scale.

Once all of that is understood, the trailer producer can go on to composing music.

Composing Music

First, the producer needs to understand that composing music can be done. He needs to recognize that music-making has evolved passed the quilt-pen and the reams of staff paper. It has moved on. Or, at least, there are other alternatives to just "writing" out music in musical notation. There is a concept that will aid the trailer producer greatly in understanding, even visualizing music.

That is the concept of MIDI, which stands for "Musical Instrument Digital Interface." As Swift defines it in *"A Brief Introduction To MIDI,"* it is a "technical standard that describes a communications protocol, digital interface, and electrical connectors that connect a wide variety of electronic musical instruments, computers, and related audio devices for playing, editing, and recording music." A MIDI connection carries multiple messages from a keyboard to the computer's interface, translating them into digital data. This is true both in the tactile sense of receiving and transmitting a piece of data from a keyboard, and in the storage of that data. A file can store MIDI data. In short, MIDI is a way that a computer can interpret music.

Even shorter, it is a way for the trailer producer to "see" music as something other than notes on a staff. It is a communications protocol for visualizing music in a form other than musical nota-tion—thereby eliminating the need to even understand standard musical notation. This is best seen in the computer program "Synthesia," where instead of musical notes, a keyboard is laid out at the bottom of the screen, whereupon any note that is triggered, a bar representing that note is correspondingly sent "up" the screen.

This is especially helpful when a previously "written," "composed," song is loaded up into the program, played, and seen. The notes "played" (herein played by the computer itself) are translated from the notes on the keyboard to blocks rising up the screen. In short, the process shows exactly which notes on the keyboard to "hit," how long to press them, and in what succession.

An understanding of any song that has been translated into MIDI can be grasped very quickly by this visual transformation into MIDI.

The trailer producer downloads this program, uploads a song that he admires, and watches which notes have been pressed to create the effect of the song. The music, of course, is not played with soaring instruments. But instead, it is played with a lone piano, breaking down the complexity of the song into a single instrument. It is meant to provide a direct and literal—at least, as literal as possible—translation of what notes make up the arrangement of that song. Notation is not used. Symbols are not used. The 'A' key simply sends up a block signifying that the 'A' key has been pressed and has been pressed for a specific duration.

This covers two key components of music: Which note is pressed, and for how long.

The program also allows for the user to "play" along with the song, pausing until the user hits the correct key. This is especially helpful for the beginning piano player who cannot locate the correct key fast enough, or deftly enough, and to assist in building up subconscious associations for how that song is to be played. The trailer producer, or whoever is assigned to the task of making music, would do well to find a song—in MIDI format—load it up into Synthesia, and play along with that song.

It is not important to play the song "well," or play it as a finely trained pianist would in concert. It is enough for the producer to understand the arrangement—and then be able to arrange the data himself. The arrangement takes place in the DAW, the digital audio workstation, in a program like Logic X, or Pro Tools, or Ableton, Reaper, or any program that allows the usage and creation of MIDI data. This is where various MIDI blocks can be pieced together—or, as one would say, composed, or written—into a moving composition of music.

Adding Instruments

At this point, however, the music plays only through a single electronic piano. Which is not sufficient for trailer music, whereupon *many instruments* are needed to produce the song. Thankfully, all digital audio workstations come with instruments; as well more can be added through an add-on program called KONTAKT. *These* instruments are what play the MIDI files and create the music.

These digital instruments, generally, are sampled audio files of professionally recorded instruments. A musician, on the other end, has been hired to play an entire range of notes into a microphone, which is recorded, and placed into the software, so that when any corresponding note is played by the user, the trailer producer, the note will sound. The 'A' key on the piano triggers however the musician "on the other end" played the 'A' note. 'B' triggers the next note. And so on. The process is a facsimile of a professional musician playing his instrument—the facsimile process allowing each note to be subsequently arranged into the composition of the trailer producer's choosing.

The Actual Art of Composing

It is up to the trailer producer, or whoever is producing this new-ly-"written" composition, to have some idea on how to compose. Which is no easy task. How is music composed? How is it written? What are the processes involved in getting from inspiration to a finished masterpiece like Beethoven's *Fifth Symphony*?

Where does one begin?

There are multiple ways. And understanding those multiple ways demands—or at least, somewhat requires—a knowledge of how to produce those multiple ways—very quickly. Composition can begin with a "melody," then continued with a set of "chords." Composition can also begin with a set of "chords" and continue by adding on "melody."

But what do those words—*melody* and *chords*—mean?

Simply: chords are more than one note pressed at the same time—typically three. Sometimes four. Melody is what it sounds like. The quick succession of notes that aid the underlying chordal struc-ture. It is what a layperson typically thinks of as music. A melodic line has two distinct axes—pitch and time. Hewitt describes it as involving a series of pitch changes.

Chords

Chords, to give a broad definition, are what "go" beneath. They are the backbone of a song. They are the structure upon which melody is placed. Chords are to a melody (and the other accouterments of music) as a spine is to a human being. The spine of that human being is made up of a number of vertebrae, of which the chords are made up of a number of successively stacked "notes." Simply, chords can change, and they make up a "chain."

Typically chords, stacked in threes or more (although, sometimes they can be stacked in twos), last two bars of music, then change to a differing place on the harmonic structure. The phrase harmonic structure being defined as quadrants on a scale whereupon the chords are placed. It is the study of chords that the trailer producer needs to be concerned with.

To simplify before going any further, it is the stacking of notes that make up chords, and the changing of these chords that shift the harmonic structure of a song.

To understand this, it is necessary to understand *which* three notes of a chord are, and how they are made up. Put another way, it is important to know that there are two types of chords—a *major*, and a *minor*. A major chord—a happy, bright sounding "stack" of notes—is made up of whatever its base note is—say, 'C' for example. And then a counting of 4 notes to the right— 'notes' including the black keys as well. That is to say, 4 "half-steps" to the right. Then, from there—which would be the 'E' note—the player counts 3 keys—including the black keys as well. That is to say, 3 "half-steps" to the right.

That is it. That is a chord. It is the C major chord, named so because its root note is on the 'C'.

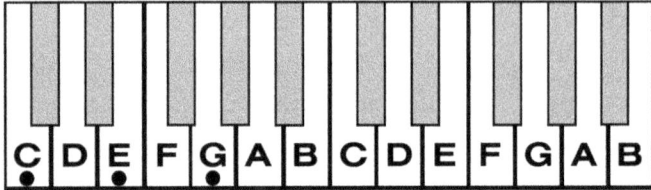

The C major chord.

This, however, contrasts with the 'C' minor chord, whereupon instead of counting 4 "half-steps" to the right from the 'C' root note, the player only counts 3. This has the effect of neutering the brightness of the major key, making it a minor, flattening it, as it were, to the point of making the chord sound tense, unresolved, dramatic. Perfect for the aspiring trailer/music producer.

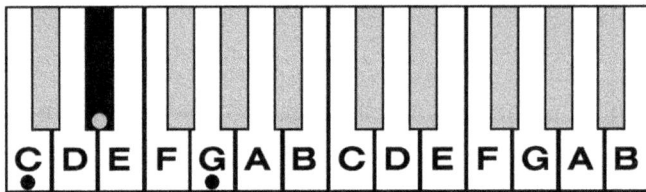

The C minor chord.

Of course, it is the interchange of major and minor—brightness and darkness—that produces the best narrative effect.

But before that, it is important to understand that only so many root notes can be found in any given scale. Continuing with the example of the 'C' chord, the player, looking for the next "chord" in the scale, would think to move to the 'D' key. Assuming the player is looking to play in a minor sense, looking for a dramatic feel, he would run into a chord whose third note does not fall within the minor scale.

The D minor chord. It is not in key and shouldn't be used.

And that is the premise to chord structure. The musician making sure that each corresponding note is played in scale, in key.

[To save time, the reader is to know that the '#' sign means "sharp." The 'b' sign means "flat."]

'D' would not make for a good chord, as neither 'D' major, nor 'D' minor, land in the key of 'C' minor. A major 'D' would be 'D', 'F#'(which is not in key, and said "F SHARP"), and 'A'(also not in key).

However, 'D#'—which is just the black note to the right of 'D' (at least, in this key)—would be the start of a good key. Only because 'D#' major ('D#', 'G', 'A#') is in the key of 'C' minor.

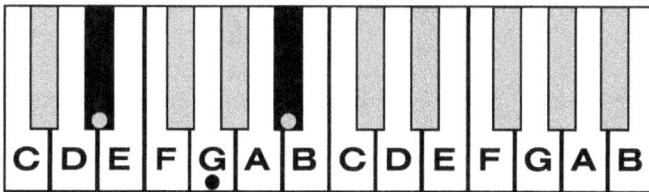

The D#/Eb major chord.

The next chord is found on the root note of 'F'. That chord is a minor, made up of 'F', 'G#'(which is just the black key to the right of G; at least, in this key), and 'C.'

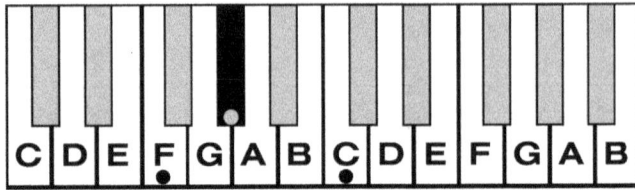

The F minor chord.

This is 'F' minor.

The next chord is found on the root note of 'G'. That chord is a minor, made up of 'G', 'Bb', and 'D'.

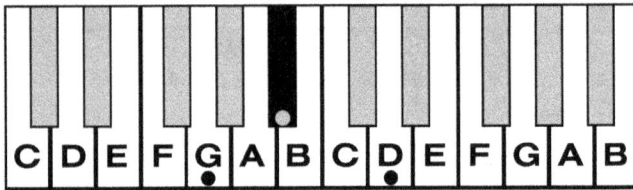

The G minor chord.

This is 'G' minor.

The next chord is found on the root note of 'G#'. That chord is a major, made up of 'G#', 'C', and 'D#'.

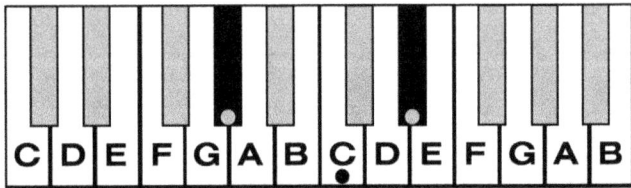

The G#/Ab major chord.

This is 'G#' major (said, "G SHARP major").

The next chord is found on the root note of 'Bb'. That chord is a major, made up of 'Bb', 'D', and 'F'.

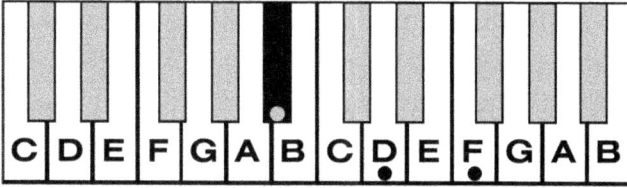

The Bb major chord.

This is 'Bb' major (said, "B *FLAT* major").

A pattern is recognized here. And that is the pattern of there being a chord within each of the root notes—with exception of the second key in the scale. In this case, it was the 'D' note.

It is the numbering of these root notes that unlocks the secrets of chordal structure in a harmonic relationship.

Each successive root note is defined as a roman numeral: I or i (depending on whether it is major or minor), II, III (or, iii, if minor), IV (to define the fourth major) or iv (to define the fourth minor), V (to define the fifth major) or v (to define the fifth minor), VI (to define the sixth major) or vi (to define the sixth minor), VII (to define the seventh major) or vii (to define the seventh minor). That is, in summary, I, II, III, IV, V, VII, VIII. That is what every scale, key, is made up of. Roman numerals based upon which root note is first pressed, and thereupon which chord—major or minor—is built.

Pressing these chords—and their respective notes—is what creates the underlying harmonic structure of the song. The producer, overwhelmed by the previous description, would just have to start trying out chords, realizing that the order they are played in is the way they will shape the song. For instance, playing i, iv, VII, and Vi, will result in a certain sound. As will i, VI, i, VI produce another.

What order then is correct? Answer: whichever sounds best to the listener. Note that the two examples are presented in fours.

This is the typical number of groupings for chord progressions. As well as is 8, 16, and 32. In short, chord progressions are created in fours, then added to in multiples of fours from there. Typically, progressions are only four chords, less often 8, even less often 16. Their order, to reiterate the original point, is largely dependent on how they sound in succession. Their "correctness" largely dependent on upon aural qualities, and the function for which they are being designed for.

This then begs another question: given the overwhelming permutations of even just a four bar chord progression, given the overwhelming time pressures on the trailer producer, what are the best orders for the chords to go in? Thankfully, trailer musician and teacher Richard Schrieber offers several patterns.

His first, already noted above—i, VI, i, VI—is a simple repetition between two chords. A back and forth. Playing them on a piano will immediately alert the listener to their familiarity and use. *They sound dramatic.* They create a musical groove of highs and lows. To use them in the reoccurring example of 'C minor', the exact chords pressed would be 'Cm', 'Ab', 'Cm', 'Ab.' That is, to put it more succinctly, i = Cm, VI = Ab, i = Cm, VI = Ab.

The idea of chordal numbering becomes even more clear with the next pattern: i, VI, iv, i. This is i = Cm, VI = Ab, iv = Fm, i = Cm. The roman numerals are always replaced with a chord selection. It is the ordering of the roman numerals, once translated to actual chords, that produces the various "sounds."

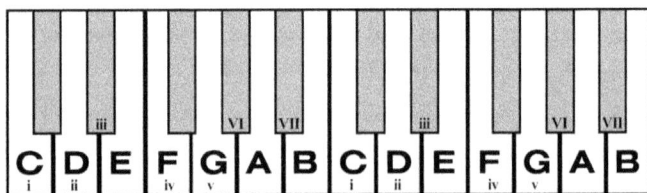

Roman numerals mark the chords of the scale. Use
this diagram for reference in C minor.

Richard presents further patterns for study.

- i, VI, iv, VII. i, VI
- i, VI, VII, v
- i, VI, iii, v
- i, VI, v, VII

Notice that they all begin with the roman numeral "i." That is, within in the example of 'C' minor scale, they all begin on the first chord of that respective scale—the 'C' minor chord. Put simply, most of the patterns listed by Richard move from the 'C' minor chord to the 'Ab' major chord—then to another chord.

To write another way, the usage of patterns here suggests that chordal patterns, while at first glance seemingly infinite in order, generally return to a reoccurring few chordal progressions. They tend to start on the first note of the scale, they typically progress to the sixth note of that scale. In other words, the patterns, the formulas, can be applied to different scales, and still work.

It is all, mostly, the same.

Of course, there are some generic principles. For one, it is generally just best to start on the root note of the scale. At least, for the trailer producer. From there, chords tend to move to the sixth. Whichever chord is used next, it typically leads back to the fifth—which generally always leads back to the first. That is, written another way, the fifth note on the scale is generally the second most "strong" note which always, aurally at least, will naturally—again, aurally—beg a return to the root note.

Only a certain number of chord progressions are possible when designing chordal progressions.

One doesn't need to fret with infinite variations. Only certain ones will sound "good." That is, certain one's "lead" the ear naturally from one to the other. Practically put, the chord patterns lead the person viewing—and subsequently hearing—the movie trailer from one moment to the next. That is the essence of excellent trailer music. It leads the listener to the next moment in the trailer. That is what is of most importance. The chords provide an underlying structure to move the trailer along in its duration. Why these chords sound right is a matter for another study, a musician's study. It is simply enough, for the purposes of trailer creation, to know that chordal progressions—and how to do them—are what provide the narrative thrust for the music of the trailer. The function of chords is to produce a skeleton.

Chord Variations

From here, it is a matter of processing out a variation of the patterns listed by Richard Schrieber. The processing done in a DAW program like Logic, usually, by parsing out the MIDI notes. Which can be manually inserted, rather than played. The first, best, notes to insert are the bass notes. These are the lowest (that is, to the left on the piano) notes in pitch. This is a matter of taking the root note in each chord—and only the root note, as anything more will muddy up such a deep sound—and moving it down in pitch. It is in producing the base notes, and then chords, programming them in, playing them, that the trailer producer, the editor, whomever is engaged in this process, begins to naturally hear space—and need—for other sounds.

Namely, melody and the subsequent construction of the song.

Melody

Melody, to be direct, is a matter of the musician listening to the chordal progressions and then playing in what sounds "good" to the listener. That is it. Of course, an art goes into it. But on a practical level, the level for creating movie trailers, it is a matter of playing something until it sounds good, moving the music along in a logical manner. Logical meaning the listener does not note the passage of time. This art, this ability to "play along" with chordal progressions, will come directly from the trailer/music producer having played the scales so many times.

Ideas for melody will come naturally, provided the proper scale-practice has been done.

Instruments

Once melody has been secured over the chordal progressions, it is time for the producer to pick out instruments for his or her composition. While a lot goes into picking instruments, and therefore placing them in a symphonic space, music production, from here, unfolds in a logical manner. First, take the chords. They will demand the expression through strings, perhaps horns. Melody will demand the expression through 'shorter' strings (shorter in that their duration is shorter), perhaps a piano. It is what sounds good to the listener. Sometimes it takes both strings and horns. Sometimes winds too. Sometimes synthesizers. Sometimes these are all playing the same note in harmony. Sometimes not. What is important is that the producer have the musical background to begin structuring this opus, and then from there, using his natural talents to guide the way.

Arpeggiation

Additionally, there are musical tricks to add more interest to any composition. First, arpeggiation—or arpeggio. This the repetition of a series of notes. Its repetition giving a familiarity that moves the piece along. The most famous example is the theme song to *Stranger Things*. Which is just C-E-G-B-C, repeated over and over again.

The beauty of arpeggiation is that it can create the appearance of musical competency, and it can be done relatively easily—provided one finds a pleasing order—which is not terribly difficult. Arpeggiation, for the lay person, is best done with some sort of programming device. In Logic, it's called the "Arpeggiator." The user simply must load it up, hold down a few notes, and listens as the computer plays those notes in quick succession. The quickness controlled by a dial marked in fractions—1/4, 1/8, 1/16, 1/32. The user will note that the increasing of these fractions (or, in mathematical terms, a decreasing) makes the music go *faster*. These fractions, of course, are how fast the music is playing within the beats per minute. A lot can be found by simply pressing on the keyboard and then adjusting the speed in which the computer plays those notes. Still further, a lot can be found by adjusting *which order* those notes play in; and even still further, a lot can be gleamed by adjusting the velocity in which those notes are played. Velocity being the manner of how much pressure is applied to the individual note itself. Harder will result in more intensity, lighter will result in less. In an arpeggiation program, this usually can be adjusted manually.

Pads

Another musical trick is the usage of "pads." These are typically synthetic sounds (although, not always), that are inserted beneath the music to "pad" out the sound. They add interest. They add weight. They bring about a greater sense of depth to the music. This is accomplished by taking one of the chordal notes and then playing along within the scale of the song. The player will note that many variations of interest can be performed by simply playing along or deviating from the song.

Percussion

Perhaps the greatest trick of music—although musicians would argue that it is not a trick, but a fundamental part of music—is the art of percussion. This is what moves a song along. It is what is most memorable and useful in the entire ensemble. It has the greatest effect on the piece itself. And as such, it is both the easiest and most difficult to get right. Easy because it is so natural. Hard because of its seemingly open-ended nature. You can play anything, really. So long as it sounds good. Much the same could be said for the other tricks of music.

The producer would be wise to just focus on what is easy about percussion. Not hard. That is, not trying to be too original with it. Instead, the producer should just use his instincts—and the guidance of the computer program. That is to say, arpeggiation, surprisingly—and perhaps much to the chagrin of classically trained musicians reading this—is a great way to plug in a coherent drum pattern. The producer should just let the computer do it for him. Simply, load up a library of drums, turn on whatever arpeggiation program is available, and press down the keys. Something will play. And, given the parameters of the arpeggiation program being in sync with the master clock of the program, something will play in time with the song's beats per minute. And, given the nature of simply playing in time, it will sound fairly good and germane to the song itself.

What Music Really Is

Not getting concerned with originality is the producer's best friend.
Not being concerned with blowing the doors off what has come
before is paramount. Further still, it's important to remember what
is being attempted. Music to aid in the moving along of an advertisement. This is not music to perform in an auditorium or arena.
This is not music that will be played on the radio. It is, in fact,
music that is highly functional, designed to underscore a commercial message, and punctuate, at various points, important parts of
that message. This is also not to remind of the earlier sentiment
that music, once clobbered beneath all the dialogue and sound
effects, once placed in a trailer, is barely, consciously, recognized
as music. Which is why so much time was spent distilling chordal
production. It is in the chords that the producer need be most
concerned with. The additions are merely icing on the cake. The
additions serving to further clarify and direct the purpose of the
piece; the additions serving to add more depth and weight, and
put honestly, contribute more misdirection, and direction, to the
listening experience.

Again, this is not music designed for a dance hall.

Of course, music production—the art of layering out the sounds
which play the composed music—is an art unto itself that could
fill volumes of books. The previous treatise was not to circumvent
or preclude a deeper understanding of musical harmonics, and
therefore music production as a whole; it was to highlight that the
fundamentals of music are a lot less mysterious than what they first
seem. The trailer producer can spend as much time with music
production as he needs or wants. He can spend as little. This treatise

was designed to get the producer thinking—and realizing—that music is a neighboring continent to the land of video editing, and that travel between the two are more possible than one would think. Through the study of notes, scales, chordal production, melody, arpeggiation, pads, and percussion, the producer has the tools to further explore and understand the art of trailer music.

A Method of Study

To better study the art, the producer simply should identify a popular trailer song (or at least, one that is current), place that song in a DAW, identify the beats per minute, then identify the "lowest" pitched sound of the piece. This will be the bass. The producer should ignore all other sounds in the piece—the arpeggiation, the pads, the melody, the percussion—and just focus on the bass. Then, identify *which* note is being played. This is best done by having a piano handy, and playing a succession of lower pitched notes, trying to match up the harmonies with the sound of the bass. Not easy. But not essential to get right. The act is to simply identify the bass note, and therefore the possible chord being played, which will be either major or minor. The benefit is in understanding that a chord is being played, and that it is being played for a certain duration, before switching to another chord. This will re-enforce the importance of chords. This will, whether done in an exact, correct fashion, direct the student to subconsciously assume the usual chordal uses. It will unlock the key of the song. Because once the student finds the first potential chord, he or she will better understand what the next chord will be, and therefore the third and the fourth, understanding that there are generally only four chords. This will then lead to the realization that the pattern is repeating, and that it is in fact a *pattern*.

From here, the producer should list each chord as it "appears" based on the bar in which it's played; he should list how long it sustains. He will see reoccurring numbers. Again, musical sections move in fours, eights, sixteens. No professionally produced song will deviate from this structure. Seeing it repeatedly provides comfort to the student/producer, and a confidence that music is not just a mosaic of impulses; instead, that it is a finely structured, logically created piece of work.

5

SOUND DESIGN

Sound is the most important aspect of a movie trailer's design. The trailer producer needs to make an entire study not just of sound, but of the body's relationship to sound itself. She must recognize that sound is not just noise, but that, through its correct usage, "becomes communication (Sonnenschein 2001, xix)." It is communicating the underlying ideas in the trailer itself. The trailer producer must understand the unique power of sound, and its effect on the listener's conscious and subconscious mind.

The Categories of Sound

A sound's qualities break down into the categories of rhythm, intensity, pitch, timbre, speed, shape, and organization (Sonnenschein 2001, 65). Rhythm marks sound through time. Intensity characterizes sound by energy. Pitch is defined by a spectrum of frequencies. Timbre is made of harmonics. Speed is how fast or slow that sound arrives. Shape is the sound's envelope, which is defined by growth, duration, and decay. Organization is how a collection of sounds are ordered against one another, making up their intelligibility. Then, the trailer producer must understand what to do with sound. She must understand the different uses of sound in a trailer, how they break down into four types, and how those four types must be observed.

Rhythm

First, rhythm. The trailer producer must understand the rhythm of the sounds being placed in the trailer. Is it rhythmic or irregular (Sonnenschein 2001, 65)? Rhythmic sounds offer a predictable tempo, repeating one after another; they are either mechanical like a clock or organic like breathing. Irregular sounds carry no sense of predictability—conversation, crowds, a volleyball game, for instance (Sonnenschein 2001, 65).

Intensity

Sound "is measured in energy increments called decibels [dB]" (Sonnenschien 2001, 66). How loud, or how quiet is something? The intensity of air is barely audible at 1 unit of energy, almost slipping by undetected. A jet taking off ratchets that number up to an almost unbearable—for some—ten trillion units of energy. A trailer should be an oscillating rhythm between loud sounds and the relative benign intensity of dialogue. Overall, the trailer should have as intense of a sound as humanly possible.

Pitch

Knowing that sound occurs on a spectrum of frequency, not necessarily volume, is crucial. The spectrum of frequency, as with music, operates in pitches (low and high), and within a logarithmic band between 20hz and 20,000 kHz. A sound's frequency has either a low characteristic, or a high characteristic. Meaning, it is either falling on the "low end" of the frequency spectrum, or the "high end," or somewhere in the middle. Understanding this is paramount. 20 Hz, for instance, would be the sound of an earthquake. A deep rumbling. This is a "low end" sound. 20,000 kHz would pass brilliance, brightness, sibilance, air and into the limits of human hearing—simply, the sound of a "high pitched" hiss. These two bands represent the spectrum of the auditory experience. It is on this spectrum that the sound designer lays her canvas. It is crucial to understand these sounds in terms of "lows," "mids," and "highs." They cover both frequency and pitch; pitch being something that a trailer producer might understand. A trailer's sound design features a number of sounds in the lows, mids, and highs, all making up the frequency of the audio spectrum.

Timbre

A characteristic of sound, timbre is the tone quality or color of a sound's noise. Timbre is how the frequencies of a sound are working together, creating either a pure tonal sound, or a noisy sound (Sonnenschein 2001, 67); the more the frequencies work together, the purer the tone will be, the more even the timbre is. Simply, some sounds are more or less noisy than others. The sine wave on a synthesizer, often used for bass, is a pure tonal sound, whereas an explosion is a "messy," noisy sound with many overlapping frequencies at play.

Speed

How slow or fast a sound travels makes up its speed. A sound can travel slowly through time, or it can progress quickly. This is highly dependent on the surrounding material in which the sound is traveling through. For instance, sound travels slowly through a concrete wall. Through the air, sound can move much more quickly, depending on the temperature.

Shape

A sound's shape. This is "defined by its shape (onset, growth), body (steady-state, duration) and decay (fall-off, termination) (Sonnen-schein 2001, 68). A sound begins, holds, then ends. Its beginning is known as the attack. How fast it takes the sound to get up to its full amplitude—or how slow. A gunshot has virtually no attack, as it arrives quickly, whereas the sustained note of an oboe would have a long attack. A sound's shape is especially important for the trailer producer and sound designer. Simply, it's important to know how long it takes for a sound to get up to speed. An explosive sound, for instance, would be used to impact a certain sudden event in a trailer. Whereas a riser, for another instance, would be used because of its slow attack, its creeping nature, rising up to climax a particular section. This concept also applies to instruments. A guitar pluck has a fast attack, a string has a slow attack.

Organization

This is how a signal is organized regarding the listener. This ranges from organized to chaotic (Sonnenschein 2001, 70). Organized sounds come off as pleasing, relaxing. Chaotic sounds break through the calm—a jackhammer, for instance (Sonnenschein 2001, 71). Sound has either of those effects. They can please or disrupt. It is up to the trailer producer to determine which effect—and make no mistake, both are necessary—is used.

Now with an understanding of sounds, the trailer producer proceeds to understand the various natures of that sound in trailer design.

The Usage of Sound

Because trailers are not a matter of lining up simple sound effects to mirror whatever is on screen, because trailers must use a kind of non-diegetic sound that reflects what is not onscreen—or heard by the characters in the trailer—the trailer producer and sound designer must make imaginative leaps toward what is ultimately being heard from the soundtrack's design. Indeed, the soundtrack of a trailer must be designed. Not just through music, but also plain old sound. And that sound has to denote meaning that aligns with the communicative underlyings of the trailer's subtext, a subtext encircling everything from story to genre. It's in this subtext where the sounds of a trailer will be found—not in its surface. It is not enough to link up an image of a gunshot with the sound of a gunshot. It is a matter of relating an image of a gunshot with the sound of a canon firing, of a lion roaring, of a tanker exploding, of a Jaguar pouncing for its food, of a door slamming shut. The two—image and sound—are separate ideas; but juxtaposed together, they create a third, aesthetic meaning. Furthermore, it is a matter of understanding the denotations conferred or communicated by a certain idea as highlighted in the trailer. What emphasizes a certain moment? What drags the trailer in a different direction? Indeed, a single sound of a certain intensity and timbre will alter the entire meaning of a trailer and send it in another direction. Great care has to be given.

The Four Types of Sounds

Upon any viewing of a trailer, it would seem that the variations of sound effects are limitless—there are booms, brams, whacks, smacks, hits, hybrid hits, risers, cracks, slams, massive hits, etc. The list could go on for pages. Furthermore, the applying of these sounds could go on ad infinitum, placing them willy-nilly through-out the trailer, wherever they seem to fit "best." A big boom sound could go anywhere in the trailer. But inevitably, a big boom should do something. All sounds in a trailer should *do something*. Because if a sound is not assigned a purpose, the sound itself will create its own meaning, dragging the trailer to its heart's content. The trailer producer must understand what purpose each kind of sound is serving. The sound in trailers breaks down into four categories, each informing a different use. The four types of sounds in a trailer are stops, impacts, accents, and risers. Each one performs its own role. Stops sever all action in a trailer. Impacts hammer home a certain point. Accents break up some of the quieter moments. Risers pad the trailer, signaling the end of a section.

Each sound does something.

Stops

The most important sound in a trailer is the "stop." This sound brings the trailer to a halt. This is the record scratch, the low thud, the large boom; although it can be anything that signifies some large change has occurred. It is used after some major value charge in the trailer has shifted. In the trailer for WONDER BOYS, when the Frances McDormand character announces she's pregnant, a gong is heard, breaking the silence, upheaving the Michael Douglas' character's life. A stop serves to literally stop the trailer and send it in a new direction. It should cease all movement, energy, and momentum.

Impacts

The next type of sound is the "impact." This is the boom, the hit, the whack, the slam—just to name a few. This the most heard sound in a trailer. It emphasizes that something important was just said or done. This is the yellow highlighter of sounds. In the trailer for ZODIAC, the one character says, "He gave himself a name"—then there are the sounds of lights flashing on, of a breath. These two sounds, combined, are impacting that moment. Another example is in the trailer for DEAD SILENCE when the character says, "There was only ever one suspect: Mary Shaw." The hit of a drum rings out as the trailer shows a nefarious picture of the Mary Shaw character.

Accents

The third type of sound is an "accent." This serves to break up some of the quieter moments of the trailer, and to emphasize—but not totally—a certain aspect of the trailer. Continuing with the DEAD SILENCE example, the one character says, "There's an old ghost story around here about a woman named Mary Shaw." Since this is not a hugely important moment, the trailer breaks it up with a quick, reversed cymbal sound. The trailer producer wanted to make way for a greater impact in the following moments. This is what differs an accent from an impact—using a sound to underline something, but still making way for some bigger reveal. Because if an impact is used too often, it wears out its welcome. All these sounds are relative to one another. Use a stop too much, the stop becomes an impact. Use an impact too often, the impact becomes an accent. Impacts and accents must be used interchangeably to keep from wearing the other out. Reverse cymbals, ticks, snips, pings, are just a few examples of accents.

Risers

The fourth type of sound is a "riser." This is a continuously rising-in-pitch sound that generally goes from one step of the musical scale, to the next. It "pads" a section, and serves to speed up the action just before the next sequence. It can be synthetic, in that it's made on a synthesizer, or it can be organic, in that it's made by instruments rising in pitch. An orchestral riser is used—among many—in the first trailer for THE DARK KNIGHT just after the Joker says, "And here we go." It is getting the audience ready for the next section of the trailer. Consider risers as cable suspensions on a bridge; they provide support to the impacts, which are the pillars of a bridge. Typically, they link one stop sound to the other, ultimately unifying each sequence together.

The four types of sounds in a trailer are stops, impacts, accents, and risers.

A Method

Before implementing these four types of sounds into the trailer, just dropping them in and figuring out which ones will work best, it is important to open a digital audio workstation and then pick out a series of synthesizers that will act to signify these sound functions, to find literal stand-ins. It goes like this: the trailer's structure is first built up with a series of electronic beeps and boops, creating a soundtrack of signifiers rather than a final rendering of what will be. These sounds are indifferent to any characteristic other than signifying that they are in fact different. The 'stop' sound might be some sort of synthesized slam. The listener knows it means STOP. The impact sound will be somewhat like the stop, but just slightly higher in pitch. It should say, "impact." The next higher pitch sound should be an accent. Then, the riser should just be a tone that continuously rises in pitch. Next, those electronic sounds will be exported back to the video editing workstation. This soundtrack will be known as the DATA track, which signifies the underlying structure of the trailer. Then, back in the audio workstation, all tracks will be muted, and the metronome will be turned on. This sound alone, the sound of a ticking metronome, will also be exported, and imported into the video editing station. It is what the trailer editor will ultimately edit to. The process will allow the trailer editor to not get bogged down in picking all the variations of sounds, leaving his attention on future picture-editing, leaving the finalizing of individual sound effects for later.

Conclusion

In summary, sound is the most important element of a trailer's design. It will influence everything about the trailer's structure, and ultimately, everything about the finishing touches. While full of inspiration, sound is not a random act, but a reflection of strategically placed choices informed by a knowledge of sound, what those sounds mean, and what to do with them. After understanding all the aspects of sound—its rhythm, intensity, pitch, timbre, speed, shape, and organization—a trailer producer, editor, and sound designer—whether they are all different people, or the same—must either pick music, or create it; then she has to understand the different signifiers of each type of sound—stops, impacts, accents, and risers. It is only through understanding these signifiers that the trailer editor can place them effectively against the dialogue, stopping the trailer when necessary, impacting when pertinent, accenting when necessary, rising to speed up and unite different sections, and then begin editing to something other than just the random inspirations of sounds; editing both to a data track and a click track. This will ensure maximum effectiveness with the most creativity and the most inspiration allowed.

6

EDITING

The Invisible Art

Editing is the art of cutting together disparate images into a cohesive whole. It is the act of making complete what was once not. The editor reviews all the material, typically shots, and assembles them into scenes, sequences, acts, and ultimately, the finished film. He makes these decisions based on the script, based on production notes, based on the director's input, based on his own intuitions—his own gut reactions. There is little else. Because while an entire century of film work reflects a robust understanding by all who have officially participated, only a vagueness remains about how it was all done. As a result, the field of editing is marked by ambiguity, hesitancy, and a nostalgia for soviet-era propagandists. It is known as "the invisible art" for a reason. It is so invisible that no one notices it.

Make no mistake, it is an art, and an art that must be mastered. But where to begin? There is no simple answer to what is good, what is bad. Cohesiveness is an important factor. Coherency, another. The story must be told, must be told well, and must be told in a logical sense. Logic, then, is an important ingredient. But logic, alone, is not enough. It is not sufficient to simply say that a piece must be logically put together, with character 'A' entering here, then character 'B' entering there, talking about this, talking about that. Something has to inform the choices made. More is needed. Comprehension, for one. Saliency, for another. Unlike film, the trailer editor must make his art completely visible, as the trailer is a vehicle for the edit. A trailer producer, editor, must cut for attention, for effect, for sales. He must shock, excite, motivate. Fundamental principles are needed, if only to inform the exact choices that must be made in the trailer editing process. The invisible art, to the trailer editor, must become completely visible.

Overview

A trailer editor must collect his shots, then organize them into "impacts" and "pictures." He must then know what to do with these shots, how to weave them together, and what principles should inform the process. These principles are established by some well-known editors and theorists, such as Sergei Eisenstein, Lev Kuleshov, Walter Murch, and Richard Pepperman. They are the principles of when to cut, of what effect to cut to, how to cut, and where to cut. Simply, a cut must be made not only in the blink of an eye, but in regard to the blink, to the movement, and must be done so within the realm of montage.

First, an organization of the collective film has to occur. The trailer editor has to divorce himself from any previous understandings about what makes up a trailer. He has to do away with any preconceptions about how he should make his selections. Common thought would dictate that the trailer editor simply look for "trailer-worthy" shots. And yet, what makes for "trailer worthy" shots might all together confuse and misappropriate what is really at stake. Indeed, what are trailer-worthy shots? How does one find them? What are they marked by? Are they simply explosions? Shots that inspire awe? Shots that excite and tantalize? What, after all, is something worthy of a movie trailer? A deeper understanding is needed. More specifically, an exact understanding is needed, and it's needed within the context of organization.

Organization

The trailer editor must categorize two types of shots—*IMPACTS* and *PICTURES*. These are the only two he need be concerned with, locating them, categorizing them, then structuring them into the overall trailer. They are indeed what make up the essence of "trailer worthy" shots. They are images motivated by psychological principles. First, "impacts" are shots that will ultimately accent and lend some sort of impact to a piece of dialogue that was just said. They are characterized by shots of collision. That is, two objects connecting, a person punching another person, someone kicking in a door, a hug, a kiss. Second, "pictures" then are characterized by shots that while interesting, are simply interesting unto themselves; they serve no other function other than to provide movement to the next impact, to highlight some potential juxtaposition.

Impacts

Impacts are the primary shots to be concerned with. The trailer editor goes through the entire film, seeking out any clip where a collision of some sorts occurs. A collision being marked by two objects connecting. These shots will be used to impact, to emphasize, a certain piece of dialogue. Therefore, they have to "grab" within a split second. And shots that "grab" are where two objects collide. It can be any type of collision, so long as it is something colliding. It can be related to humans: a kick, a kiss, a punch, a hug, a handshake. Or it could be objects connecting—a car slamming into another car, an explosion, a gunshot, a window smashing, a light turning on. Anything where two objects collide, and therefore grab the attention of the viewer. These shots will be used to emphasize and exclamate.

Pictures

Pictures are the next type of shots the editor needs to find. They are anything but collisions; and yet, they are marked by distinguishing characteristics. First, movement. Second, contrast and difference. Shots with the most movement are of chief concern to the editor. He must be concerned with these because it's movement that most motivates the human eye. An object suddenly moving on a plane will draw more attention than an object that is static on the same plane. This is called "winning the competition for saliency" (Itti L.; Koch C, 2000). The human eye, watching the trailer, will move directly to the most action. Therefore, shots with movement take precedence. The editor must find images that show movement—running, jumping, waving, turning—even something as simple as a smile could, in the right context, be sufficient. Then, shots with the most contrast are of the next importance. This is a little more difficult to deduce as it is not so obvious at first glance. The shots with the most contrast are generally the shots of most differential in their composition—lines heading in different directions, angles jutting (not to be confused with camera angles) at varying degrees, differing shapes breaking up the composition, colors clashing (or, in color theory, complimenting). Contrast. Difference. A building standing against a clouded skyline. A woman against a brick wall. A car against a background of straight lines. White on black. Blue and orange. The screaming red blaze of a sky as a dusk sun sets in front of it. Anything with contrast and difference will make for a good "picture," will make for a good inclusion in the trailer, will make for a future, interesting juxtaposition, will make, ultimately, for a "trailer-worthy shot."

Admittedly, pictures can bleed into becoming impacts. A picture of a sunrise, in the right context, could serve as a magnificent "impact." Although, the reverse is mostly not true. Impacts, by their very nature, by showing an event of collision, will draw attention to itself, and therefore "impact." They should be kept separate.

Collection

The editor should scroll through the movie looking for impact and picture shots, parsing them out to their respective bins. It is best if the editing program used allows the user to scroll, indeed be able to view shots on the fly, so the editor does not have to sit through the entire film, waiting and wishing to come across other shots of collision and movement. These kinds of shots are noticeable at a glance, and best noticed at a glance. Too much movement (such as the general movement of watching a movie) can obfuscate actual, legitimate collision, motion, differentiation, and contrast.

Editing

After finding as many shots as possible, and loading them into their respective bins, and not taking too long to do either, the editor turns back to the data track as previously created. Simply, he cues the track up to the first impact sound. He then searches through the 'impact' bin and picks a shot that is most relevant to whatever piece of dialogue is adjacent to it. He then places the shot over the impact signifier. He repeats this for each subsequent impact sound. This will create an effect of hearing the dialogue, then suddenly seeing some sort of collision on screen.

Juxtapositions

When it comes to choosing which impact shot to use, the editor is most concerned with creating what are called juxtapositions. This is the effect of two adjacent items creating a third—in our case—'intended' effect. The concept was coined by Soviet film-makers Sergei Eisenstein and Lev Kuleshov. It is a dialectic leap that creates a new qualitative attribute (Eisenstein 1949, 72). A hidden meaning—which is obvious to the viewer; hidden in that the effect is typically felt, perceived. The picture of a man, looking. Then, the picture of a woman. The two shots create a third effect: what the man must be feeling looking at the woman. The effect is a juxtaposition created by the two shots. It is this effect that the trailer editor repeats again and again, searching through the impact folder, and then layering down impact shots against the impact signifier. The effect will be created by the dialogue and then the subsequent shot of collision.

Consider the example of a typical James Bond trailer. The soundtrack introduces the voice of an ominous villain who simply says, "I imagine a world…without war." The trailer cuts to a shot of a car exploding. The voiceover further adds, "I imagine a world… without suffering." The trailer cuts to someone clasping their hands, silently screaming at the sky. The voiceover continues, "…I imagine a world…without harm." The trailer cuts to two men punching one another. The voice finishes by saying, "I imagine a world… without James Bond." Suddenly, on this note, the trailer cuts to the famous gun barrel point-of-view of James Bond, flashing his gun at the audience, shooting.

That would be a well juxtaposed trailer. Everything that the voice says is contrasted or outright contradicted by the images shown. The more visceral these juxtapositions, the better the effect on the audience, the more engaged they will be.

Simply, pile on the juxtapositions.

It's in the collisions where pure moviemaking is found. It's in the collisions, juxtaposed against the dialogue, where most trailer moments will be discovered.

Of course, with experience, the trailer editor, drawn to creating juxtapositions, will discover that movies—especially low budget movies—offer a dearth of direct impacts to create such striking juxtapositions. It's the unique challenge to the editor to find these moments. Most movies are lacking in distinguishable instances—collisions. Or, in other words, most movies would have been better off as stage-plays or novels.

Next, the trailer editor will select from the 'pictures' section. These images will overlay the holes where, whoever is saying the dialogue, is not shown. For instance, if a line of dialogue says, "Hi, I'm Jackie Brown," and Jackie Brown is not shown saying that, then a "picture" of an image of Jackie Brown doing something—anything—hopefully something visual—will be shown. It is easy to imagine a shot of Jackie Brown turning in the direction of the camera or opening a door. Anything that says, "Here is Jackie

Brown!"

While the impacts were to directly juxtapose whatever was being said, the pictures are to illustrate, to illuminate, are to compare what is being said in that exact moment and vicinity. It is important that the trailer editor not get hung up on picking the exact, correct shots. An approximation is needed. The editor will usually be surprised by what works, and what does not.

Montage

What's important is that the trailer editor edit, indeed, select, images based in this framework of juxtaposition, and then work from there. How long the shot lasts will be determined by the click track (or even the music); the content will be determined by either juxtaposition or illustration. Beyond that, all of trailer editing can be reduced to the ideas explored by Sergei Eisenstein and his concept of "montage." He listed five kinds: Metric, rhythmic, tonal, overtonal, and intellectual. All of which are used in the art of making movie trailers.

Consider metric montage. The montage—the edits—are constructed based on a metric beat, which Eisenstein called "giving a clarity of impression" (Eisenstein 1949, 73). This is why the editor first spent time on constructing an exact tempo track—it was to give clarity of impression.

Rhythmic montage, in contrast, goes beyond using the click track, and instead looks at the actual content within the frame of the shot. Cutting from a woman turning to a turning man creates a certain rhythm; as does cutting from that same woman to the shot of someone firing a gun, creates a separate rhythm.

In further contrast, tonal montage is concerned with the tone belied by the edits. It is more complex than just cutting to a rhythm;

rather, the effect is to draw out emotions in the viewer; the trailer cuts from two people kissing to a man machine-gunning a crowded room, then cuts to a shot of someone breaking down in tears. The effect is emotional.

Then there is overtonal, which is tonal, plus all the actual effects of metric and rhythmic, creating a meaning beyond emotion, creating a "collective calculation of all the piece's appeals" (Eisenstein 1949, 78). This would be making all the cuts as previously listed, plus cutting to a shot of a man, punching the air, backgrounded by a looming American flag. The effect is emotional, plus intellectual. What it means is up to the viewer.

What The Movie Wants

After "dropping in" the impacts, pictures, and making the necessary tweaks to pacing, the editor must sit back and watch the trailer. Which will be an exceptional experience; because if the method was followed, so much information will be thrown at the editor. The data track will beep and boop, the juxtapositions of the dialogue and impacts will startle, and the images will illuminate meanings that were not there before. The effect will overwhelm. This is important. It shows that the trailer is doing its job—and that is, to overwhelm. But it is also important because this is the trailer speaking to what it wants. Simply, this is the movie speaking across the duration of its own runtime. *This is what the movie wants.* This is what the movie has always wanted—and wanted to say.

It is important that the trailer producer, at this moment, just take it all in. It is crucial that the editor replay the trailer, then do so a few more times; do so until the overwhelming results wear off. Because it's after the effects diminish that the trailer editor will start to really understand where the next round of edits will need to take place. It's where the trailer editor will be able to listen to what the movie trailer actually wants. This, ultimately, is what's first and foremost when editing a movie trailer. What the trailer wants. Not what the executive or trailer dispatcher wants, not what the director wants, not even what the editor wants. Indeed, the ultimate authority when it comes to movie trailers is the trailer itself. It will tell where to make the cuts; it will instruct on where to refine those cuts. The editor has done the hard work of researching through the film, finding the "best" moments, then layering in those. It's then up to the trailer to instruct on how to best proceed.

Editing Concepts

Thankfully, two editors supply insights that will help with the finite, final editing. Walter Murch with his theory about the blink of an eye, and Richard Pepperman with his theory about cutting on maximum motion—on the blur.

Blinking Eyes

First, the Murch theory. In his book *In The Blink of an Eye,* Walter Murch proposes an experiment of filming an audience—but done so in infrared, so that only the eyes of the audience are visible. This would create the stark effect of seeing a ramp of blinking lights—eyes, refracted by the light, blinking in the dark. The theory supposes that the blinking of the eyes would instruct if a movie is working or not. Simply, the more erratic and out of concert the eyes are with one another, the less the movie is working. If the eyes are blinking in unison, then a collective effect is occurring, and the movie is working. However, it is not the blinking the theory is concerned with; rather, it is the thinking that is bellied by the blinking; it is the thought process betrayed by the blink of an eye. Therefore, edits, on screen, are best performed just before or after the person on screen blinks. This is to confer that the person on screen is almost ready to think about something else, and therefore a new piece of information should be introduced—before or after the blink. The editor uses this knowledge to her best ability. She should never cut on a blink—that is, right when the person on screen is in the middle of transitioning to a new thought. To do so would scatter the blinking of the audience, and thus, their thinking. The theory is proposed to keep everyone on the same page. The effect of following the theory is to keep thought moving in a linear motion, keeping everyone watching engaged and in concert.

To reiterate: the editor should always cut before the blink, never on it.

Cut On the Blur

Second, the theory by Richard Pepperman in his wonderful book *The Eye Is Quicker*. His theory postulates that editing is best when it is most invisible. That is, when it is unseen by the audience. Therefore, the best editing is done when the most motion is onscreen. Or, in other words, when the action moves so fast, the image, the visage, blurs. Pepperman advises to cut "on the blur." The movement will trick the audience into seeing something else, leading their eyes right into the next shot.

These two theories will aid the editor in making any refined cuts.

Final Editing

Further help is up to simple trial and error. The editor will have to lengthen shots, then shorten them. Some impacts, some juxtapositions, really, will be too soon; that is, their effects will be excessively sudden in the trailer's runtime; other juxtapositions will come too late. They should build least to the greatest.

The editor will have to sometimes vacillate between using hard cuts and "soft" cuts. That is, sometimes simply cutting from one image to another will be more apt; whereas, sometimes, he can use what is called a "dissolve"—one image blending into another. The dissolve, an effect, covers a great deal of poor editing. It can also convey the passage of time. Additionally, some edits that would otherwise be fine are disturbed by a loud sound, an impact or an accent. The editor has to make allowances and adjust accordingly. Also, the song will offer some dictates. The editor, again, has to work with the entire effect.

It is important that the editor not agonize over exact shots. Rather, the editor should just "feel" for the correct usage. When it comes to trailers, there is no correct shot, or correct juxtaposition. It is a matter of what collection of effects the trailer should offer the viewer. In the case of selling movies, that is the effect of huge, mounting interest, paid off with the desire to actually see the movie. The editor should not worry about "giving too much away." He should instead ponder the overall, cumulative effect of the trailer itself.

In conclusion, the editing of a trailer is the work of finding, selecting, and stitching together dissimilar elements of a film. The editor must understand the principles of editing, of the basic concept of placing one image next to the other. Then, he must go through the entire film, searching for the best "shots"—best defined by practical photographic and psychological concepts—selecting those shots based on whether they are an "impact" or a "picture. Then, he must use the principles of juxtaposition and montage to place those selected shots onto the data soundtrack created earlier. In refining the edits, he uses trial and error, keeping mind of the "blinks" and blur of motion, cutting on or around those concepts. All of this will amount to a finely edited trailer, one that will captivate, entrance, inspire and motivate an audience.

7

COPYWRITING

Sales In Print

At some point in a trailer's design, a storyteller, a point of view has to be introduced. This is the classic narrator, the trailer voice saying, "In a world where." This is a perspective being affixed to the piece. Sometimes this is referred to as coming up with a "cool" tagline for the film. But the word 'tagline'—let alone the word 'cool'—does not begin to capture what it means to affix a point of view to a trailer, and then introduce what that point of view is in fact saying to the audience.

In other words, a trailer, as a sales piece, needs to be coupled with a salesperson. That is the ultimate point of view of every trailer—a salesperson. It is not from the artist's, it is not from the director's, the producer's, the writer's, the banker's—whomever is involved in the project. It is the point of view of the salesperson. And as salesperson, the "tagline," the words that flash up in the course of a trailer—whether they are spoken or just written—must be from the point of view of the *interested* salesperson. And as such, the words must not only be heavily influenced by an interest in the film's success, but by a deep interest and study in the art of copywriting. The taglines seen in trailers, the words that must be written, are actually called "copy." As in *copywriting*. It is what's used to sell cars, jewelry, vacations, books, entertainments, and all sorts of products. Copywriting is what's used to sell soap.

A study of movie taglines is the study of copywriting.

Because it is through copywriting—writing copy—movie copy— that the ultimate selling job of the trailer is done. Not through the edits, not through the sound or music. It is done through the medium of either a narrator speaking out instructions, or copy— actual, written copy—flashing up on the screen, directing the viewer's thoughts and emotions.

Of course, the copy will not be as upfront as, "Buy now!" At least, not while the trailer is being introduced to the market. That kind of direct sale is usually saved for home video—of which the filmmaker, especially today's filmmaker, might want to consider. But for now, we need to be concerned with "the soft sale." Not the direct.

The copy will guide the viewer along, nudging them toward viewing the trailer. The copy is to set up a parameter, say what the film is, offer some sort of poetic, rhetorical device to remember the film by, and then name the film. Whether this is done by narration or simply words—or both—is up to the trailer producer, or the financial backers—mostly the financial backers.

As such, the trailer producer—now trailer copywriter—must turn to the greats of the field of copywriting. Before writing a single sentence, the trailer copywriter must divorce from the world of the visual, turn back, survey a hundred years of the field itself, and read everything. She must read Dan Kennedy, Gary Halbert, David Ogilvy, John Caples, Drew E. Whitman, Eugene M. Schwartz,

Robert Collier, Ted Nicholas, and others. Doing this will give the copywriter an appreciation of the field itself. No longer will the aspiring movie copywriter see "taglines," or "slogans," but instead will rather see instruction, words assembled for a single purpose: to sell movies. It is the job of the movie copywriter to become a successful salesperson. She is the first line of defense in selling the film to the moviegoing public. And the sales job, the writing of copy, is not to be taken lightly. The words, the copy, will carry the movie itself. And they have to be seen as *words*, not as visual cues. Learning to write is key.

Take for instance the opening chapter of the first serious advertising book ever written—Robert Collier's *The Letter Book*. The chapter headline is, "What Is It Makes Some Letters Pay?" (Collier 1931, 1) That is an intriguing question—especially for the financially-interested party who is looking to make their movie pay. The producer must simply swap out "letters" (an old word for advertising) with the word "trailer." What is it that makes a trailer pay? The shots? The music? The story? The sound? The actor's names? In essence, it is the summary of everything, as written about through copywriting. Collier asks, "What is there about some letters that make them so much more effective than others?" He answers, "Bait." Like a fisherman applying a lure to a line, it is the job of the trailer producer to craft more effective bait than the next movie-in-line. To apply here, it is the job of the movie copywriter, to sum up the essence of visual and sound and provide a compelling sales-job for the viewer to see *this* movie—and not that other movie.

Not to denigrate, but to elevate. This must be the Most Important Film Ever Made. Which is why movie taglines—movie copy—tends towards slogans like, "Get ready," and "Prepare for." It is the point of view of the trailer, the salesperson invited into the theater, the room, the whatever, that the presentation at hand—the trailer—is a sales vehicle for one of the most ultimate film-going

experiences known to man. No matter the movie. No matter its
quality. Simply, no matter. Like the dedicated "company-man," the
trailer copywriter must get behind everything in the trailer and
the movie, sum it all up, and sell, sell, sell. She must create bait to
see this movie, and this movie alone. And what will sell a movie?

Simply, the promise that this is the best movie ever.

Or, at least, that this movie, about this particular subject, is the
best movie ever about that subject. If it were a film about zombies,
about the horror of zombies taking over the world, then the trailer
would promise an experience to end all experiences—about zombies
taking over the world. Simply, this is the best movie ever about
this subject. It is the job of the trailer copywriter to capture this
experience, to sum it up—as it were—to encapsulate it somehow,
with emotion and reason, pathos and logos, and "pitch" it to an
audience member. Doing so, and doing so through old-fashioned
sales techniques, is what makes the job of copywriting so difficult.
There are only a few words in the trailer, but they are a difficult few
words. Difficult because of brevity. Difficult because they must do
so much. Difficult because they must encapsulate so much.

It is the job of the movie copywriter to represent all of this.

Therefore, it is imperative that the movie copywriter understand
what she is trying to sell. Not in vague terms. But in actual, demon-
strative, actionable copy. *This movie is great because it is about this,*
says the trailer. To subsume that, the copywriter must understand
the actual movie. To do *that,* the copywriter must step back and
survey the experience.

It is not enough to say, "This movie is swell." The copywriter
must reduce the film to its most important elements. Journalisti-
cally, this is the who, what, when, where, and why. Take for example,
MARTY, a 1955 film starring Ernest Borgnine about a lonely city-
man searching for his better half. No easy sell. In the official trailer,
famous actor Burt Lancaster is enlisted to introduce—literally,

by standing before the camera—the picture. He starts off with announcing that the movie takes place in New York City, what that place is like, and that there is a man who lives there named Marty, who, for the simple reason of this all being introduced, is special, and that, on a Saturday night, is finding difficulty getting a date. The actual copy, as read by Burt Lancaster? "It's the story of a Saturday night in a man's life." The narration—the copy, really—serves to introduce Marty's problem, why he has the problem, and how that problem is going to be solved.

Problem, solution.

The Sales Job

Movie-copywriting is all about selling a story. Not the intrigue of it, not the mystery of it—but of its simple existence. The audience wants to know that a story—any story—is about to unfold.

How it unfolds is of very little consequence. At what level this is done is dependent on how articulated the expectation is needed at that given time. Take for example the first teaser to the THE DARK KNIGHT RISES, where anticipation would have been in the nascent stages. The teaser, shown a year before the film's release, is a basic montage of sound and image, a juxtaposition of a city crumbling with contextless dialogue from the film's characters, and contextless shots of the characters, mostly looking tense. The clarity of specificity is purposely dialed back. First, the teaser begins with writing: "Every hero has a journey." And then, "Every journey has an end." The propositions are that 1) a story about a character is about to be told. 2) The story about that character will come to an end. The rest of the trailer, even though expressed in dialogue, is copywriting writ large: The commissioner Gordon character says, "We were in this together, and then you were gone. Now this evil rises." He finishes up by saying, "The Batman has to come back." With the teaser aiming toward evasiveness, the promotion is coaxed out by copy, even though that copy is said in the form of dialogue. The Gordon character is delivering what would have been the copywriter's job. It is doing the same work as Burt Lancaster was doing in the MARTY promotion. In this case, the exposition delivered by an actor is copy enough—is information enough.

But information has to be given in some fashion, and it has to be given in the form of character, setting, value, and antagonism. Even the most opaque of teasers has to make definite promises. The audience simply wants to know that an unfolding of story will take place with certain characters in a certain location, with certain conditions, and that a certain form of antagonism is going to either keep it the same—or make it worse.

Of course, how this is done, this totality, is up to the trailer producer, and, when delivered to the copywriter, is often a matter of subsuming what is actually there in the trailer. Of having the story, as expressed by the trailer itself, make sense. *A story must be sold.* Therefore, movie copywriting is the reduction of a film's *setting, character, value,* and *antagonism.* Character, because the audience needs to know where to localize their feelings; it is after all about the same kinds of people sitting in the audience. Setting, because the audience needs to know where this takes place. Value, because the audience needs to know "what's at stake." And antagonism, because something will stand in the way and fill up the duration of a motion picture.

No matter how oblique, no matter how mysterious the trailer aims to be, the trailer, the teaser, the advertisement, must promise definite setting, character, value, and antagonism, and therefore the copywriter must bring alive, and make definite, those qualities. This promise is either done through writing, narration, or, in more modern contexts, the speaking of a character in the film. It is up to the copywriter to pick up the weight of the trailer and coax out and make definite the film's story. It is the copywriter's job to make everything understandable.

It is up to the copywriter to make those promises through clarity and salesmanship.

Character

The copywriter first examines character. Consider the final trailer for THE DARK KNIGHT RISES. It is a trailer tilted heavily toward, and obviously, its central character: Batman. Whether on purpose or because the marketing team felt the story was not germane enough, or whether everyone involved just wanted to retain a sense of mystery, much of the film's actual plot is left unsaid. Instead, the following lines of copy are used as a direct sell

1) "On July 20"
2) "The Epic Conclusion"
3) "To The Dark Knight Legend"
4) "The Dark Knight Rises." (The title serving to name the movie, while suggesting what will happen)."

The title cards lay out a single proposition: On July 20, the audience will get to watch the highly anticipated last act to the previous installment of THE DARK KNIGHT—a 2008 blockbuster that ended on a cliffhanger—and will find out what has happened to Batman, and what is going to happen to Batman. This is a simple proposition, and an even more simple sell. It is also a promise. This installment will be as good as the previous. *This will be as good as* THE DARK KNIGHT, simply because Batman is about to return.

Setting

Second, a copywriter uses setting. Take, for example, the trailer to Robert Altman's NASHVILLE. The eponymous nature of the film suggests a certain location. The trailer funnels everything about the film through the lens of NASHVILLE being about people living... in Nashville. The copy, as spoken in form of third-person narration, extols, "NASHVILLE is about a lot of things and a lot of people." The narration is referring to the film's title, but the words double for setting. This is a special motion picture because it is about people living... in Nashville—its very uniqueness because a movie is being made about these people, a kind of postmodern take on the nature of film itself. It is the copywriter's job to supply narration to explain this. The copywriter is saying, with words whether printed or verbally spoken by narration, "You should focus on THIS."

Value

Third, a copywriter highlights the film's value charge. In the trailer for THE SUM OF ALL FEARS, the copy, as performed by a third-person narrator, announces, "At a time of increasing tension..." This spoke directly to the mood of the culture when THE SUM OF ALL FEARS was released in 2002, just months after the terrorist attacks on the World Trade Center, Pentagon, and Shanksville. The copy is of a writer highlighting a certain mood, or, in this case, a certain value: safety. THE SUM OF ALL FEARS is about a country on the brink of war. The trailer shows images of jet fighters, security-bureaucrats, dark offices, questionable politicians making Big Decisions, nuclear weapons, computer screens, vehicles crashing, soldiers, subterfuge, and disaster. The dialogue underlying these images is of curiosity, apprehension, announcement, discovery, of political intrigue. The copy is written to centralize everything around that very specific mood of, "Something bad is about to happen." It is the job of the copywriter to make definite what the trailer, or even, the movie, whether deliberately or by accident, has made oblique, opaque, vague. It is the copywriter's job to artfully (and that word is loaded) look at the summary of the trailer, step back, and say, like any good salesperson, "This is a remarkable motion picture. It's about x, y, z, and because of that, you should watch it." This localizing around a value speaks to what advertising expert Drew Eric Whitman in his book *Cashvertising* calls the Life-Force 8, which describes the eight biological desires of human beings (Whitman 2009, 21). They are listed as,

1) Survival
2) Food
3) Freedom
4) Sex
5) Comfort
6) Superiority
7) Protection of loved ones
8) Social approval.

The copy for THE SUM OF ALL FEARS speaks directly to survival. It is describing a value charge, and in an artful, metaphorical, way, how that value may be overturned. Here, it is about a country at the edge of the War on Terror, a singular mood that defined an entire decade-plus of American living. Contrary to speculation by critics that Americans would not be ready to see depictions of terrorism so soon after the 9/11 attacks, THE SUM OF ALL FEARS opened at number one, and eventually went on to gross $194 million dollars.

Antagonism

Fourth, copy is harnessed and influenced by the pressure or pressures of antagonism in the film. Take for example the 2001 movie HANNIBAL, which heralded the return of one of the screen's most memorable villains: Hannibal Lecter. The trailer for HANNIBAL is, as one might expect, all about Hannibal. As if not covered enough by the dialogue spoken by the film's characters, and words spoken by Hannibal himself, the trailer hands it off to the copywriter to really hammer home what this film is about: "HIS GENIUS."

"HIS EVIL," says another title card, in red, bold, bloody letters.

The trailer is about, as the final card says, "HIS NAME... HANNIBAL."

The copy of the trailer then asks a question, "How long can a man stay silent […] Before he returns... to do the thing he does best?" Which is then juxtaposed by a silhouetted shot of Hannibal carrying an unconscious woman. The copy finishes up the job by hinting toward the film's plot: This is about the return of Hannibal Lecter, how long he takes to come back into everyday life, and what he is going to do once he gets there. The copywriter makes this abundantly clear, setting up expectation for a film about Hannibal's epic sojourn from Florence to invading the life of the film's hero, Clarice Starling, once again.

The copywriter, through character, setting, value, and antagonism, captures the essence of a film's story, and makes clear what has been left unsaid by the trailer. The copywriter's chief job is to sharpen, refine, hone, enhance, polish up, and elucidate what is only artistically hinted at by the trailer's choice and arrangement of dialogue. Most times it is up to the copywriter to clarify what is oblique, or what is all together missing. A story. The hard truth is that most movie copywriters will have to, for all intents and purposes, re-write, or all together create, a story that may not be there. It is often left to the copywriter to make this final "lay-up." It is up to the copywriter to harness together all elements of story and polish up, in an artful way, what may have been only implied by the trailer itself. It is the copywriter's job to bring in directness, direction, and a conduction of the final orchestration.

8

TITLE DESIGN

[The following chapter is as software-agnostic as possible. The designing of a copy's text is usually done in a program called After Effects. Of course, it can be done in Apple Motion, or any other compositing program. It can also be done in the video editing program used by the editor of the trailer. In fact, it will more than likely be up to the video editor to design the copy's text—so the following words will be of great import.]

Creating Titles

It is not enough to just type out the words of copy and spray them across the screen. They must be befitting of the surrounding trailer's quality. Or, put in other words, they have to reach the level of artfulness appropriate to the surrounding trailer. They have to stand out, while at the same time, standing in. They have to meet all the qualifications of solid graphic design, while at the same time, blending with the surrounding product. Written words like, "In a time when the world has gone dark," must at the same time signal the viewer to read them—legibly (another important qualification)—but they must not be too "outstanding" to distract from the adjacent aesthetics.

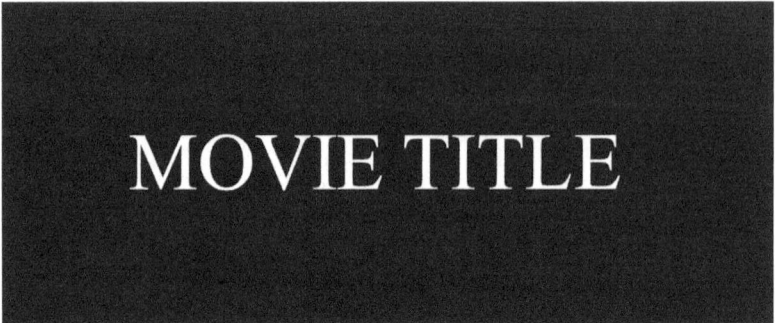

A title without design. This is how basic text looks.

A title WITH design.

To reiterate, written copy in a trailer must not be simply written out. It must be structured, designed, and ultimately choreographed through the unifying principles of graphic design. With the text alone, correct fonts must be chosen, the respective font size—regulated—kerning adjusted; leading, tracking, baseline shifts, vertical and horizontal sizing, alignment, all must be considered so one can finally land on a satisfactory result. Then, color. Is the text white? Black? Grey? Is this accounting for the different shades between pure white and pure black? This is not even to calculate for the hue, saturation, and brightness of a color—all of which must be carefully weighed against not only the surrounding image of the text, but of the neighboring trailer. Simply, the colors have to "match" the rest of the trailer in a pleasing manner, they must be "weighed" as if holding some sort of invisible weight. It is not just differences in hue that will make a character of text stand out—it is the weight, the depth it achieves when considered against adjacent colors.

The Background

A background image must be selected. This is where the difficulty of the work skyrockets logarithmically; if work is done to the text, then corresponding, even greater work must be done to the background image; which in turn demands work be done to the text; which in turn repeats the process. Both placement of text and the background image have to then be considered against one another. What is the text's alignment in contrast to the background? Does one affect the other? The "rule of thirds," must be implemented. All these components will just barely scratch the surface and, just barely, render a pleasing result of static text on a background. This, all, is to say nothing of actually moving the text. That requires an individual inspection of going back, looking at how the text can then shift against the background, or how the two can migrate about as one.

Font

The trailer producer, the artist, really, would do well to set a basic line of text against a black background and consider only the "look" of the text—its font. Deriving from the Middle French word *fonte,* "[something that has been] melted; a casting," it is the look and function of a piece of text. A font is derived of its weight, style, and width. Its weight is judged by the thickness, a font ranging from light to ultra-bold. Its style can be standing up right or slanted. Its width can be compressed or extra wide, or anywhere in between.

In any program, the baseline font will be what's called Times New Roman, or Arial.

These two fonts are what most people are familiar with. And generally, just as a matter of them being the default, are not to be used—at least, not most of the time. This requires mentioning because some video editors, forced to do the titles, will simply use the first font that is available on their computer. This is not good practice. If Times New Roman is to be used, it is to only be considered after a vast casting of other fonts. Because it is a *casting*—a cast call—of fonts that must be done. The user, the artist, must first scroll through all the available fonts, sometimes choose one, then select another, then compare. It would be very possible to have upwards of ten strings of type on a screen, all saying the same thing, all with differing fonts. It is that essential of a process.

Many Types of Fonts

There is a galaxy of fonts, all with differing weights, styles, and widths. Of course, these are organized based on five classifications: serif, sans serif, monospaced, and display.

Serif fonts are, as David Carson in his Masterclass on graphic design states, fonts that, "evoke feelings of history, tradition, honesty, and integrity." This is Times New Roman, Times, Garamond, among others.

Sans-serif fonts are like serifs, but without the defining serifs attached to the ends of the fonts. A great example is Arial.

An example of monospaced would be Courier—the classic

typewriter font. All the characters in this font occupy the same amount of horizontal space (Rosendorf 2009, 12).

Display fonts are everything else. These fonts are created to be shown at large sizes.

In any event, all fonts are funneled through these five classifications.

The Usual Suspects

While there are many fonts, movie trailers tend to come back to the same types again and again. Of course, Times New Roman is top of that list. But so is Trajan, especially Trajan Pro. Then, of the sans-serif variety, Arial, Helvetica, Futura. In recent years, a reoccurring font is Agency FB, which has upwards of 17 variations. Then, the geometrical typeface designed by Aldo Novarese in 1962, Eurostile. These fonts tend to be shared among the genres, but some of them are better suited to one than the other. For instance, Trajan Pro is perfect for serious dramas. Although, it is also perfect for action and horror. Of all the fonts, Trajan Pro is perhaps the most ubiquitous, used in such film trailers as SAW.

Agency FB is often used for science fiction, as it was only designed as recently as the early 90s; it tends to say "futuristic, and 'present-day." Examples include MAD MAX (2015) and ZERO DARK THIRTY. Designed by David Berlow, it is a close cousin of his font, Bank Gothic. Sometimes, Eurostile is used for sci-fi—but it belongs mostly to the action variety, used in films like WHITE HOUSE DOWN. It is a font specifically designed for headings—or, here, trailer design. Futura, another geometric creation, is about efficiency. It is seen in a variety of works, used mostly by Stanley Kubrick, David Fincher, and Wes Anderson. Examples in film are GONE GIRL, SKYFALL, and GRAVITY. The ITC family has been used recently to connote and evoke the 1970s and 1980s horror films of John Carpenter—most notably used by the show *Stranger Things.*

An entire book could be written about fonts. Especially fonts used for movies, as some fonts are more "cinematic" than others. To really understand how deep the topic is, the trailer producer should write out a line of text, and then select and view that text through each font.

Size

From here, the correct font size must be chosen. Large, small? Compared to what? Font sizes range from 6 to the hundreds. Titles can take up an entire screen, or they can be as small as the viewer can still perceive. Scope comes into account—only so much can fit on the viewer. Legibility must also be considered; the artist must consider what the average distance the viewer will be from the final viewing-screen. Then there are the other matters of a font's characteristics.

Tracking

Tracking is a major concern. How far will the individual characters, within the entire title—and uniformly—be spaced? How close? Excessive margins between each character says something about emptiness, a closeness says something else about—well, that is up to the viewer. It is very subjective.

Kerning

Kerning, as contrasted by tracking, is the individual space between characters, in so much as some characters can have more space between them than other characters. This becomes especially important when writing something like "AV," as the edges of the 'A' and the 'V' take up more space on their respective top and bottom than is visible to the naked eye. It is important that these do not take up anymore white space than is necessary. This is affected by the practice of kerning, the process of adjusting the spaces to create a proportional and pleasing result.

Leading

Leading concerns with the space between each line of type. Sometimes it's best if the trailer producer, the artist, just exact this by eye rather than try to shift within parameters; although, leading is most helpful when dealing with three or more lines of text.

Baseline

Conversely, baseline shifts are how the bottom of each word is placed against a similar reference point on that leading line. This is to adjust how each word fits horizontally with its neighboring word.

Proportion

Font can also be sized horizontally and vertically, each individually of one another. Proportion is important when considering whether to have 100% horizontal and vertical. Proportion causes perceived effects. An increase in one axis or another creates a disjointment, a paranoia. It is best to use horizontal and vertical sizing in small increments, as it is a matter of total proportion.

Alignment

Alignment is the setting of the type relative to the page. Center alignment is usually used. Although, left or right placement, relative to one side of the screen or another, can be used with great effect.

These are all parameters that must be judged against one another, refined, and re-dialed in. These parameters, the totality of them, creates the basic and intentional—or unintentional—effect, result, of how the text actually looks. Simply put, font selection, size, tracking, kerning, leading, baseline shifts, horizontal and vertical proportions, and alignment, all effect the sum of font design.

Suffice to say, the trailer producer would be wise to look at all the fonts in the genre of their trailer and deduce some commonalities. The same ones tend to be used over and over again. There are rules.

Surveying The Images

Before color is added, it is important to judge the simple, basic shapes of the font, and its various characteristics, against the adjacent images—both of what background will be used, and the images of the trailer. For now, it's a matter of looking at the images of the trailer. Does the font match? The artist must consider proportion, shape, line, and texture.

Proportions—Again

First, what are the proportions of the dominant images in the trailer? Are they big images, or small? Or somewhere in between? Does the trailer highlight images of vast landscapes, towering spires, sweeping galaxies? If so, then the proportions are large, and a large type design would be beneficial. Conversely, a small type design might bring attention, and make larger the surrounding images. It is a matter of juxtaposition. The artist must ask himself the effect he is going for. There are shades such as 'irony' and 'consistency' to consider. A sci-fi film could consist of spaceships sailing against a black, star-studded space. A small type, one with generous tracking, could speak to the emptiness of space—despite its vastness. Or, blocky, tightly packed letters, something from the Eurostile font, could speak to the technology, to the boldness of space travel. It is very subjective.

Shapes

Second, what are the shapes that make up the images of the trailer? Squares? Circles? Triangles? Are geometric figures typically represented in the film's images—as would be in a sci-fi picture; or is this a drama where shapes are typically made up of people, of talking heads, of landscapes? "Swoopy," as John McWade calls it.

Lines

Third, what kind of lines are there in the film's images? What is the general direction of the picture? Right angles? Obtuse angles? Straight lines? Curvy lines. Again, a film with many natural landscapes would speak to multiple lines and therefore lend itself to the serif variety.

Textures

Fourth—are there any unique textures in the film? A movie filled with technology would speak to the geometrics of Futura or Eurostile, or, for a tighter effect, FB Agency. This idea is also related to the literal textures found in the film, as well, the more metaphorical textures found in the story's rhetoric, in the story's genre. If horror—and therefore chaos, bloodshed, abominations—then a fraying of the title might be in order. Of course, the film may be based on a book, and therefore the texture speaks directly to the usage of a serif; especially if the film is based on a book of horror.

Simply, the artist needs to ask, "What typeface goes with that?" (McWade 2010, 35) A chosen typeface must express something, and then express that same something in relation to whatever is surrounding it. Typically, this will be the film's images. Ultimately, it may be whatever background is chosen for the typeface. Whatever is selected, whether it is chosen for a consistent or ironic effect, it must be chosen deliberately—not randomly. It must, as art critics are fond of iterating, "Say something." Here, it must speak about the ultimate effect of the trailer. Because, in many ways, the typefaces are the ultimate effect, and final say, of a trailer's design.

Color

Then, a color must be selected. This is done through the dimensions of brightness, hue, and saturation. This is no easy choice. Simple binaries will not work. If a title is to be white, then it must be a shade of white—depending on its saturation and brightness. If a title is to be black, then it must be determined on what shade, on what level of saturation and brightness, is the best fit. Usually, an all-white color looks tacky. Conversely, an all-black title looks equally as crude. Both suggest that the artist has no idea about the actual dimensions of hue, saturation, and brightness.

The Background

Finally, the artist must choose a background of some kind. A picture, whether static or moving. It is generally something related to the movie, such as a texture or shape. It can be located either directly behind the text or pushed further back in 3D space. Because, in fact, a piece of text, once the background is considered, must be considered in 3D space, as most motion graphics softwares have the capability to move about in that manner. Regardless, the artist has to think in 3D space. Is this background something like a single foot behind? Or is it 100 feet? Of course, the computer doesn't register "feet," or typical metrics, but instead measures in pixels and coordinates—x, y, z axes.

What is important is that the artist understand that since he now has the text, he also has to place it onto something; thereby creating a "space" of some kind. It is best to establish what kind of space that is. Even better if that space is determined either figuratively or literally. Figuratively in that text can exist against a black background, suggesting somewhat of a vacant space. Or, that same text can be placed against a black background, can be haloed, spotlighted by a 3-dimensional light, creating a vignetting around the text, suggesting that the text is on some stage some-where. Of course, once a background is added, the whole effect changes. Now title and background exist as one, creating an entirely new entity—itself the title design.

Now the two work together to create a singular effect. Text must be re-worked against the background; the background must be re-worked against the text. The two will share parameters like sizing, texture, color, and atmospheric effects.

Sizing

Sizing, for one, has to be done almost ad nauseam until the right proportions between the two are struck. The background must be made larger and smaller, if only to get the proportions against the text right.

Texture

Texture, another, because font and background, together, create an additional two shapes. The artist must examine how the text intersects with the background. Does it slip in naturally? Or does it create an unnecessary jagged line. That might be the effect, and therefore the artist might wish to keep it as is. Or he may not.

Color

Color, again, has to be considered. Not just of the background, but of the text—indeed a re-considering of the original color has to be chosen, as it usually will not work with the selected background.

The two—title and background—pressed together, must work in harmony. A color wheel must be consulted, as the colors must either complement, be monochromatic, analogous, or any variation of the three.

Complimentary Colors

For complimenting, the text must be one color, say an orange; then the background, must be at the opposite. The color wheel dictates that this would be a shade of blue. Incidentally, this is what most color correction results in—orangish skin tones against bluish shadows.

Monochromatic Colors

Monochromatic is, as the name suggests, a uniform of colors that share a similar realm on the color wheel.

Analogous Colors

Analogous colors take into consideration neighboring colors on the wheel.

Atmospheric Effects

Atmospheric effects, then, are sometimes added to hem in the text and background. Smoke, fire, water effects are sometimes used to add more excitement, or provide a certain cohesion between text and background. They are also used to create a specific effect. Indeed, all of those listed above culminate to create a total effect, known as "movie titles."

The titles in a trailer are the tone and voice in which the salesperson speaks. They have to be designed carefully. The trailer producer would also be wise to study the works of Saul Bass—one of the most famous and most written about. Others would include Richard Greenberg (who designed the titles for ALTERED STATES, ALIEN, and THE DEAD ZONE); Kyle Cooper (who worked on titles for GODZILLA, *Metal Gear Solid 3,* DAWN OF THE DEAD, ARLINGTON ROAD, TWISTER, and many others); Dan Perri (STAR WARS, TAXI DRIVER, NIGHTMARE ON ELM STREET, THE EXORCIST, RAGING BULL—among a host of mega-hits from the 70s and 80s); Pamela Green; and Michelle Dougherty (of *Stranger Things* fame). The study of movie titles—and their design—is inexhaustible.

A Reading Recommendation

Before any work begins, the trailer producer would best be served by reading John McWade's "*How To Design Cool Stuff.*" And then read it again. The book, while seemingly innocent and short, is one of the most comprehensive, dense, and profound books ever written on the subject. Its short length—say nothing for the title about "cool stuff"—tricks the reader into thinking that this will be a walk in the park. At first glance, of course. But with repeated readings, it becomes clear that a great deal of the book is containing all of the fundamental principles of essential graphic design. To the trailer producer designing motion graphics for his trailer, McWade's book is one of a handful of books that must be read, honed, practiced, and then ultimately, mastered.

9

MIXING

The audio of the trailer must be mixed. That is to say, the music and the effects must be set at a level where they both sound good, working together, sound loud, and yet are not interfering with the most important aspect of the trailer: the dialogue track.

Organizing The Track

This all presupposes that the various audio tracks in the trailer *have* been organized into dialogue, sound effects, and music. If not, the trailer editor must survey the entire production so far and find some way of making sure these tracks stay separate—separated especially at the glance of an eye, and the click of a button.

There are two primary ways to do this. First, the agnostic way, which can travel across all systems. All dialogue tracks are to be placed at the top of the NLE's audio section. The audio should take up no more than four to six tracks; anymore is asking for clutter. The dialogue tracks should take up the next layer; itself taking up no more than four to six tracks. As well, and finally, the music tracks should make up the third layer; itself taking up no more than four to six tracks. Each layer, as it were, should be separated by two to three tracks, so as to create a visual "bumper" between each layer so that the editor, or whomever is doing the exporting, can see that all tracks in that layer have been disabled or re-enabled accordingly.

The second way to do this is specific to Final Cut Pro X. It is a way that makes the program specifically unique, and specifically *useful*. All audio files in the timeline can be tagged according to dialogue, effects, and music. It is important that the editor do this as she goes along, or in one deft swoop at the end. Each time a clip is brought in, it is marked. Or, at the end—in a tedious fashion—each clip is re-marked to its respective nature. In any event, the audio clips must be flagged, as Final Cut Pro X allows these corresponding distinctions to be linked to a series of checkboxes marked "Dialogue," "Effects," and "Music," of which can be turned on and off.

It is this turning on and off that is of most importance. When audio mixing is done, indeed when audio delivering is done, it is of the highest importance that the audio channels of dialogue, effects, and music, be completely separated unto themselves. Dialogue should not share any "sounds" with effects; effects should share nothing with "music." They are to remain entirely separate. It is this separation that makes audio mixing possible. The editor should disable all sound, and then check each stratum individually to ensure that no sounds from the corresponding layers are mingling.

Checking The Pre-Mix

Once all tracks are separated, the editor must ensure that this is the "mix" she wants. It is here that the editor can have the most, individual control. She should play through the trailer multiple times, listening for sound. What should be heard is a loudness of music and sound, and a just-barely-audible sense of the dialogue, as the music and sound will be excavated—in an aural sense—to make room for the dialogue.

At this point, it is important to ensure that the music and sound are working together as best as possible. This, of course, would have been naturally done all along. The editor would have dialed in the decibel level of the various audio clips as they were brought in during the auditioning stage. But it is important to review, to go back, to play through, and hear if any changes can be made. Those changes will be made in two ways. Either by an accenting, or a diminishing. First, an accenting: sounds can be brought out further, made punchier, just simply by making them louder than the rest. Second, a diminishing: corresponding sounds can be made louder by lowering the volume of adjacent sounds. A punch sound can be made louder by lowering the gunshot sound that is layered in directly beneath; and vice versa. It is at this juncture these changes are to be made.

Generally, the music should all be of a consistent level, depending on how "loud" each song is. And loudness is a factor. An audio clip could claim it is at a certain volume level, in spite of it sounding completely different. It is here that the editor dials in the correct volume level based solely on her own ears. The music, when corresponding with the sound effects, will not change in volume in the mixing stage.

To re-iterate, it is important to "get" the effects and music tracks to sound as they are supposed to in the final mix. They should get along; the music making up the "bulk" of the soundtrack, the impacts heroically jumping out at their various locations. When mixed, the music will be lowered, and the impacts, punctuating the various cues of dialogue, will jump out.

Adjusting Dialogue

When the sound effects and music are set appropriately, the editor moves to the volume of the dialogue. With dialogue, audibility is most important. Not just in a uniform sense, but individually. The editor must ensure that each line of dialogue is 100% audible, both with the sound effects and music on, and with the sound effects and music off. They sound different in both contexts. A sound effect, or a piece of music, can cover up a trailing-off of dialogue; a sibilance in the actor's voice could be squashed by a conflicting frequency in the sound or music. A line of dialogue like, "We aren't afraid," could turn into, "We ARE afraid."

Therefore, it is important each piece of dialogue be individually treated and unified. First, the editor turns off the sound and music. Then she goes through the dialogue. Does everything sound OK? Can everything be heard correctly, and is it all at the same level? The audio meter can be used to judge this. Generally, dialogue should register at 12 dB. Although, this cannot account for loudness, which is entirely subjective. That has to be determined by careful listening. That listening is to be done by corresponding each level of dialogue against all the other lines of dialogue. Is there an evenness?

Then, the editor must account for lines of dialogue where the actor trails off at the end their speech—a common occurrence. For this, a tool called a "compressor" must be used. The compressor acts to flatten the loudest sound, while raising the total volume of that piece of audio. Here it is to flatten out the loudest spike in the actor's voice, thereby raising the lower part, evening it out. A listener can tell when this has been done in a movie trailer. An actor whispering can be heard against the rest of the soundtrack. The trailer for EVIL DEAD is a good example, where the actress, at the beginning, is talking about the haunted cabin they are currently trapped in. Her voice has been seriously compressed to hear each and every nuance of her speech. While an extreme example, similar care has to be given to each line of dialogue. This evenness of dialogue is to serve the editor when comparing levels against sound effects and music.

Adjusting Effects & Music

Once an evenness of volume has been applied to each audio track, the editor then turns back on the sound effects and music. It is time to assess how loud the latter two tracks are against the dialogue. Usually, the dialogue will be just barely audible. This is a signal for the dialogue to be turned up, or for the sound effects and music— and the *two as a whole*—to be correspondingly turned down. The editor has to decide which happens. Turn the sound and music down? Or turn the volume up? The split is six-to-one, half-dozen to another, but it can be determined by how loud the volume on the audio meter is creeping up. Is the audio meter registering in the red? If so, it is time to select all the sound and music files and uniformly turn the audio down.

Of course, the editor wonders how far? Indeed, what is a good volume for the sound and music to be against the dialogue? In his "Audio Mixing Master Class," on LinkedIn Learning, sound engineer and specialist Bobby Owsinski advises turning the entire monitoring system down, and then working from there, lowering and raising the music (in his class, he is referring to vocals against the music, but the effect here is just the same) so that the dialogue just audibly comes through, and everything is understandable. In other words, the editor must turn her computer's audio system down to just barely audible levels, just enough so that the entire production can be heard, and then listen, closely, to ensure that the dialogue is in fact coming through. The process has the effect of tricking the ear—which has become dulled by repeated listening—to lower all but the most important information: the dialogue.

When the volume is turned back "up," the dialogue will compete nicely with the sound effects and the music. Of course, it should still, at this point, compete. It is important that the dialogue not be wholly present against the music, hugely dominating. Because it is at this juncture that the sound effects and music be dealt with and dealt with in a matter that they allow the dialogue to breathe through effortlessly. In other words, the editor must set up conditions for the dialogue to be foremost against a correspondingly loud sound effects and music track.

The "Final" Mix

This is considered the final "audio mix." But rather than mixing, it is a matter of excavating chunks, pockets, carvings, in the sound effects and music for the dialogue to fall nicely into. To put another way, the audio is not so much mixed as it is attenuated against the most important aspect of the mix: the dialogue. All further volume adjustments will be done against the dialogue, and for the sake of the dialogue coming through.

And while up to this point "volume" adjustments have been made, the editor will no longer be using "volume"—solely—to judge and create her final mix. Instead of uniform volume, individual frequencies will be used. That is to say, pertinent frequencies of sound will be considered, and then correspondingly lowered to make just enough room—but not too much—for the dialogue.

Frequencies

First, it is again important to understand what is meant by "frequencies." On a spectrum, audio is measured in denominations of frequency. Pitch, in other words. The spectrum ranges from 0 Hz to, typically, 20 kHz. The lowest pitch is 0, the highest is 20 kHz. Simply, audio mixing is concerned more so with pitch than it is volume; it is the pitches of the dialogue that must be most apparent to the final listener; and to do that, it is important to understand what pitches—what frequencies—dialogue takes up. Typically, as defined by R. J. Baken, adult males will have a fundamental frequency from 85 Hz to 155 Hz (Baken 2000, 177). Conversely, a female's voice has a fundamental frequency of 165 to 255 Hz. But that is just *fundamental frequency,* or the lowest pitches of both male and female voices. It goes without saying that it is *fundamental* that these frequencies make it through in the trailer. This is where the "lowest" of human voices live.

Because then, the audio engineer, must be concerned with the so-called "mids" and the so-called "highs." The mids marking the middle frequencies, the highs marking the higher frequencies. Indeed, the human voice takes up most of this spectrum. What is important is to know that a base intelligibility will be somewhere in the mid-range. That is the most crucial place to lower in volume for the majority of dialogue to come through. Then, for dialogue artifacts like sibilance, it is important to lower the upper ranges, the space between 2 kHz, and 5 kHz.

That is how the final track is to be mixed. Not through writ-large volume, but by frequency. This allows no frequency to be left unfilled, allowing the dialogue to take up only what it will take up, and then leaving alone the rest. To begin, the audio engineer starts with either the music or the sound; either is fine. Then, he goes through, locating individual frequencies, chunking them as it were, and lowering them to make room for whatever is the current piece of dialogue. This is done, listening to the dialogue, on repeat, lowering that respective frequency's volume, then raising it, playing it over and over until the piece of dialogue comes through. Then, this is repeated—both for the music, and the sound effects.

It is in the transitions where the audio engineer will run into the most problems.

Transitions

The transitions, for lack of a better word, are where the volumes of each respective frequency must be turned down. How fast they are turned down is a matter of what is referred to in mixing as "attack." This attack produces either fast or slow "turn downs" of the volume. How fast, or slow, the track turns back "up," is a matter of what is referred to as "release." This is the volume returning from the turn-down to its normal level. How much the volume is turned down is entirely subjective, although, it is usually uniform across the entire piece. Turning the music down 3 decibels at one point in the track will uniformly work for the rest of the track. If the mixing has been previously done right, then it is simply a matter of locating the points of attack and release and turning the track down at those points only. This is done for both music and sound effects. Preferably, it is done first for the music, as that is going to interfere most with the dialogue. Then, it is done for the sound because there it will run into the tightness of the transitions against the dialogue. It is at this stage where impacts will come in too early (or hang around too long) and interfere with the dialogue. Again, it is a matter of attenuating the attack and release, how fast or slow the volume dips out, and then how fast or slow that dip is exposed.

Raising & Lowering

Once all the frequency and volume shifts have been made, then it is a matter of raising and lowering the volume of both the music and the sound effects track, lowering them as one, with the frequency changes in place. To re-iterate a previous point, the volumes should be attenuated so that, played at a quieter level, the dialogue is what ultimately comes through. The computer's monitoring volume is to be turned down, so low, that only the dialogue and a smattering of music and effects are heard. Again, audibility of the dialogue is of paramount importance.

Then, the system's volume can be turned up, and the final product can be played, the trailer producer now able to enjoy the "final mix."

10

MASTERING

Once the final mix has been achieved, the product itself can be, what's referred to in the field of audio engineering, "mastered." That is to say, the various elements of dialogue, sound effects, and music, are glued together as one, and then polished, as one, to play, as one. Loudness is the primary concern here. It is the goal of the trailer producer to get the trailer as loud as possible—while at the same time staying under the legal limits of 0 dB. Passing this legal limit is what audio engineers refer to as "blowing out the speakers," or severely testing the limits of those speakers. A crackling sound is introduced. It is important to retain loudness, without coming to this level. If anything, it is best to stay around -3 dB. This process can be done either manually, with individual filters, or with a program called iZotope's Ozone. The mastering engineer has to develop an ear for what sounds best—not only to his own ears, but to the ears of everyone who will be viewing (listening to) the trailer—that is to say, how the trailer will sound to those final listeners. This goes for the entire process of mastering. The trailer producer has to understand that subjectivity and objectivity are needed. Subjectivity because, "How does it sound?" Objectivity, because, ultimately, the sound will be considered in an aggregate form. There will be many people listening to this soundtrack. But primarily, there will be many electronic speakers—and many *kinds* of electronic speakers—playing this soundtrack. Large monitors, small monitors, headphones, laptop speakers, theater-level speakers, TV speakers, just to name a few.

Process

First, the process of mastering can be done manually. A chain of audio filters is applied. These filters are designed to modify the sound itself and apply a better cohesion to the final product. The primary filter placed on the audio is an EQ. To what settings these are placed at is entirely up to the discretion of the trailer-producer-turned-audio-engineer. Usually, the lower frequencies need to be attenuated a few decibels. At what frequency this attenuation begins is up to the engineer. Then, there is usually a point in the mids section that demands being lowered. Further, the highs are often raised, if only to provide an extra bit of "crispness" to the final sound.

Compressing

Then, a compressor filter is applied. While there are infinite variations for the compressor's setting, what is most important is to apply a level listening experience. The volume should be uniform. With both the louds sounding loud, and the quiets...raised in volume. Everything should be heard and heard well—without introducing too much of a compressed sound to the soundtrack, which is apparent when the soundtrack loses its sense of dynamics. In other words, the soundtrack, as a whole, needs to retain a sense of dynamics, a high and low, while, technically, just staying at the same level. No easy task. This is done with a compressor.

Maximizer

Further, a "Maximizer" is added. This tool is designed to bring out more overall volume in the soundtrack, all the while limiting the sound at a certain level—say 0 dB. As the maximizer level is set lower and lower, the overall sound raises higher and higher, creating an optimal loudness peak. This tool also adds a great deal of "coloring" to the tone of the soundtrack. Great care has to be given not to abuse this tool, as its nature can quickly cross over into the realm of compression—not to mention, *too much loudness,* whereupon it will be turned down by whomever, or whatever, is in charge of the final exhibition (YouTube installs an algorithm to turn down uploads whose volume crosses a certain threshold).

iZotope Ozone

Second, this process can be achieved via automation with a tool called Ozone. The automation process, in the program, is labeled "Master Assistant." The trailer producer simply places the filter on the track, finds a reference piece (usually the audio of another, professionally mastered trailer), inserts that reference piece into the program, selects whether a "modern" or "vintage" coloring is appropriate, plays the audio, and clicks "next." The program inserts all the necessary filters, sets the levels, and renders its final result. Of course, more tweaking can be done, and most times, must be done. But for the average trailer producer, the results will be more than pleasing, more than passable. This tool is especially useful for the trailer producer not entirely versed in the known-as dark arts of audio "mastering."

Once the soundtrack has been mastered, it is then re-coupled with the video files from the initial project.

Via the process of mixing and mastering, the final audio is taken from unpolished and jagged, to pristine and acceptable. The trailer producer first, uniformly, attenuates the volume of the music and soundtrack, adjusting the points of attack and release, adjusting the system's volume both for maximum quietness, and maximum loudness, ensuring that the dialogue remains dominant. Then the final result is mastered either manually, or through the program Ozone. The result is a professionally polished soundtrack.

11

MARKETING

After mastering, the trailer is done. Or, at least, it is done…in principle. The trailer producer hands off the trailer to the client, who in turn shares it with their people, the investors, creatives, whomever, whereupon it is attached to the film and placed through subsequent and respective distribution channels, exhibited, shown, used to advertise the film, etc., et al. In short, the trailer, more often than not, disappears. Unfortunately, more times than not, the trailer is incorrectly treated as a piece of obligatory promotion—a device that will simply find its way to audiences—or a device that audiences will simply find their way to—and not a valuable asset in of itself that needs promoted.

In other words, the *promotion needs promoted.*

Marketing, Promoting the Trailer

This chapter aims to not instruct with the making of the trailer, but with the *marketing* of the trailer, its distribution, its promotion. This chapter looks at the distribution of trailers through the lens that, in current time, it is not enough to simply have a trailer, it is that a trailer must be correctly packaged, created, then marketed, distributed, and promoted. There is simply too much clutter out in the digital ether for the trailer to become lost in for it not to be marketed, distributed, and promoted.

First, a trailer must be marketed, promoted. That is to say, its placement must be strategized. When will the trailer be released? Where will it be released? To whom will be watching it? What, in turn, are those people or entities supposed to do? It is important to recognize that a trailer must do what all marketing must do—call its user, its viewer, to action. In this case, that is the action to have someone, or some group of someones, to form expectations about the film, and then pay money to see that film. The reader must remember, a movie's box office is not accumulated in people having *seen* the film—it is in people having *paid* to see that film. The trailer, as a whole, must be marketed so that the ultimate viewers will form expectations, form desire, and then be prepared with knowledge to act at a certain time. The trailer, and its marketing, must inspire and move audiences in a correct fashion.

A Plan

Whomever must ultimately own the trailer, herby referred to simply as the producer, must have a marketing plan. And to have a plan, that producer must know what she wants from the trailer. Is this entire endeavor designed to entice an audience member. Who? A whole set of sociological questions must be asked, not to mention age and sex. Or is the producer attempting to have another producer, another company—distribution or sales representation—buy the movie (and therefore, the trailer)? Of course, a lot of these questions will be answered at the outset, at the beginning of the trailer-making process. But it is here that these questions must be answered again and clarified. Who, what, when, where, and why? The producer needs to know if they are trying to sell directly to consumers, or to an intermediary like a distribution or sales house. Or, perhaps, the producer simply wants to submit it to festivals. In which case, another marketing endeavor needs to occur. In any event, an endeavor needs to be created. That is marketing.

Direct Sales

To begin, consider that the producer simply wants to sell directly to consumers. First, the producer needs to realize that this will take time, as demand has to incubate. It is not enough to simply release the trailer on the day of the film's release. *Demand* must be created and must be created to incubate for a certain stretch of time. Simply, the trailer must be given time to gestate in the audience's mind. A window of at least several months is needed. This leaves enough time for gestation, but also not too much time for the trailer to be forgotten. It allows expectations to take root, and desire to be formed.

Distribution

Or perhaps, again, the producer would like to entice a distribution house, a sales house. Then the strategy would be altogether different. Time would be greatly compressed, as a sale, or a representation, would happen through back channels, discretely, or not all together overtly. Numbers aren't the goal. But, rather, credibility. This is a complexity not usually considered. Some distribution and sales houses do not want to take on a film that the public is already aware of, already forming interpretations and demands of. Some houses do not mind. Again, it depends on the goals of everyone involved.

A Hybrid Approach

Or maybe, the producer would like to do both. She would like to start advertising to consumers but would also like to leave open a window for a distribution house to come in, for a sales agent to arrive, or, for perhaps some other worthy acquisition like a top-tier movie studio, or a name-director or name-producer, or even a name-actor, to trounce in at the last minute and provide a fortune for the rights to the film. Dreaming must be accounted for.

In any event, time and scope must be arbitrated. A plan has to be constructed.

An Overall Plan

For the sake of brevity, consider that the producer would like to just create an overall sense of demand. Then to market toward this aim, she would have to establish an overall indefinite window of time. Instead of several months, the trailer is simply unveiled, promising an eventual release of the motion picture. The trailer is used simply to cultivate a general demand, no one—including potential distribution and sales houses—knowing when the release is to take place.

The trailer itself, then, *must be advertised.* Not just released. To correctly market a trailer, then, it is a matter of advertising the release of a trailer. Hopefully, appropriate marketing structures have been put in place prior. That is, marketing structures to alert a potential pool of audience members that indeed a trailer for the motion picture—the motion picture they've been promised for so long—is about to be "unleashed" on the general public. That is, marketing of the major motion picture should have been done long before the trailer was ever created, long before the film was ever photographed.

The art of movie marketing is an act that is not just ongoing between conception of a motion picture and its finish; it is done in the overall arch of a filmmaker's career. It is about the filmmaker, about he or she already having demonstrated content to an audience, having an audience, and creating expectations for what they will be doing *next*. In other words, the filmmaker should already have an audience waiting.

Of course, this is not realistic; say nothing for the obvious catch-22 of the situation. In most cases, a trailer will be created within a vacuum, where no audience exists. **Indeed, the audience itself has to be created.** Therefore, marketing is treated separately from distribution. Marketing is, generally, the creation of not a plan, but of an audience. As an audience must be created, because without an audience, there is no point in having a trailer, let alone a motion picture.

There is simply no point without an audience.

Finding The Audience

An audience must, first, be found. If none exists prior, if there is no future plans on creating that audience, then the audience must be, at this point, created. It must be marketed, and then *marketed to.* This first involves the setting up of a "signaling" location. A Facebook, a website, a Twitter, an Instagram, some kind of social media where people can be gathered and talked to at once. We will call this a "staging-ground." This staging ground is where the audience will receive updates about the film itself. It is here, at the staging ground where an audience is built. Because, ultimately, it is the creation of audiences that draw the attention of distribution and sales houses, festivals, and Hollywood powers—not the creation of motion pictures. Put another way: ***it is the making of audiences that brings success, not the making of movies or movie trailers.***

Once an audience is found, located, created, whatever, they must be notified that indeed a trailer has been created and that it is in fact coming out at a certain point in the future. Again, demand for the trailer itself must be cultivated and curated. It is no longer enough to simply show the trailer; the producer, the team involved, must use the trailer as means of creating an expectation to see something, anything. Demand and expectations must be created for the trailer itself.

This is the art of marketing a trailer. The planning of an audience, creating expectation with that audience, and then ultimately catering to that audience. Once expectation of a trailer is created—usually done through some kind of presented artwork—the labor of distributing the trailer can begin.

Platforms

Regardless of what the plan is, the trailer must be released on multiple "platforms." Platforms are spaces upon which the trailer will play. Various websites are various platforms. YouTube is a platform. Indeed, there are platforms within platforms on YouTube; different channels have different and varying amounts of subscribers. The producer's website is a platform. Facebook is a platform. Indeed, there are, like YouTube, platforms within platforms on Facebook. A theater is a platform—the original, in fact (although, the trailer will more than likely not play in a movie theater before a major motion picture). A DVD is a platform. As well, a DVD playing the trailer *before* another movie is a platform—a completely different platform all together.

To simplify, we must first consider the web as a platform itself. This will be the primary location where the trailer will be exhibited. First, the trailer is released on the producer's platform, where demand is most expectant. Of course, this website could be an HTML website, or a Facebook page that the producer controls. Simply, *the trailer must first premiere where the producer has the most control.* Whichever platform the producer has the most control of is the one where the trailer should begin its long sojourn.

The Gatekeepers

Then, from there, audience size and depth, should be considered. Who or what gatekeepers owns the biggest, most involved audience? Usually these are websites that cater to a specific kind of genre. A trailer for a horror film, for example, is transmitted to a website that specializes in talking about, simply, horror films. Of course, 'transmitted' is a word that suggests an unwarranted amount of ease. It will not be simply a matter of "sending over" the trailer. A great amount of begging and borrowing will have to be done. As the exchange between producer and an owner of a specific website, say, a popular horror website, is not an exchange at all—but rather, a request for access. The producer, owner of the trailer, is attempting to hijack—at least, in a relative sense—the audience of the website. Some site owners—really, audience owners—may not want to traffic in the producer's trailer, let alone her film. It may not be a part of the site's owner's plan.

Simply, the film and the trailer may **_not_** be a part of anyone's plan.

Which is why marketing will continue into distribution. The

trailer itself must be marketed to the varying nodes of supply. The trailer must be sold to people, who will in turn sell it to others. Whether that happens on a site, or someone else's Facebook, that selling must happen, and must be made mobile enough for more selling down the line. To put another way, the trailer producer has to create a viral-worthy product, a "sticky" message, as it were. This, of course, has nothing to do with the film, but rather, the message of the film. Not in any profound, or sociological, or psychological sense. But rather, message in the sense of, "So-and-so important is starring in this film, and that is why it is important." To put in still more words, it is here, at this unfortunate end, where most producers will find themselves: a movie and movie trailer that carries with it no value or impetus to be shared, and then shared again. That is, a movie without movie stars. *Without audience.*

Nevertheless, the producer must push forward, constructing a compelling enough message to the influence-holders, the gatekeepers of a potential audience. Usually, this is reduced to a matter of the film being of a certain genre. Horror is a seller. Action, another. Thriller, less so. Dramas—forget about it. If a drama, it is important that a producer re-shift the weight of the trailer to being about something enticing. That is to say, the actual message of the film has to be construed as something timely, or present. No easy task. Which is the reason most dramas never see the light of the day. Much begging and pleading will be involved in the case of dramas.

The producer reaches out to the various owners, gatekeepers, influencers, people who own sizable audiences, entities who can control those audiences through websites, YouTubes, Facebook pages, Twitters, LinkedIns, whatever social media pages that exist at the time this should be read, and asks, politely, that the trailer be transmitted through those channels, to those specific audiences. All the better if a compelling message is attached.

It is at this point a producer realizes the importance of having planned all of this out from the very beginning.

Because it is at these nexus-like junctures where a movie can either take off, or crash and burn. It is here, in the audience-building stage, in the stage of obtaining an audience, or obtaining access to an audience, where a movie begins to take flight—or crash and burn. It is through the trailer—a great trailer—what this entire writing has been about—that movie success is either born or aborted. In short, the message is either there in the trailer, or it is not. Extra pleading can be added. But usually, it is in the trailer. And it is up to the various influence-holders, gatekeepers, whether they want to share the message, the "good word," with their audiences.

The producer then works through all the gatekeepers, writing to, pleading with, to show the trailer. It is then up to the respective gatekeepers when the trailer is released. In other words, it is at this point that the trailer producer loses control over the distribution of their trailer. Which may or may not be a good thing. Like the Dorthy-device in the film TWISTER either crashing on the side of the road or being sucked up into the F-5 tornado to do its intended readings, the trailer will be either distributed or it will not.

Flight or Flop

Usually, the distribution of the trailer is a direct indicator of the potential success for the movie. Wide distribution equals wide success. Narrow distribution equals narrow or no success.

Therefore, it is of the utmost importance that the producer acquire as many platforms of distribution for the trailer as humanely possible, and then let go of wherever it goes. Because it is here, within this panopticon of exhibitions, where demand will cultivate and stew, and lead to either further interest by sales or distribution houses, or audiences themselves.

Simply, the trailer must be seen, and be seen by the most amount of the correct audience as possible. It is not enough for the producer's grandmother to see the trailer, for his or her grandparents, cousins, family and friends to see the trailer—it is that *the trailer must be seen by an audience receptive to the message in the trailer*—i.e., this is a horror film for people who like horror films, and that they should get ready.

Creating Demand

Next, this pent-up demand must lead somewhere. It is not enough to create demand, and then let the movie sit. The movie must play somewhere, and the audiences must know when and where that will happen. Is that information transmitted in the trailer? Maybe, maybe not. That is a complex matter beyond the exhibition, marketing, and distribution of the trailer. It is of our importance here to establish that demand must be created, and that it must be channeled.

All the while, the producer must keep *promoting* the trailer; must continually go through the efforts of marketing and distribution, continually churning up interest in the motion picture. It is not enough to simply release the trailer once and be done with it. The trailer will be a weapon in which the continued warfare of a film's promotion is fought—ad infinitum.

To summarize, it is the trailer through which distribution is most concerned—not the movie. Audiences will ultimately find the film, provided the proper demand and curiosity has been piqued, and has continued to be piqued. Through marketing, distribution, and promotion, the trailer producer, the producer—really—will either find success, or find failure. Whichever, is up to the producer, and to whether a compelling message has been created within the marketing and distribution of the motion picture itself.

Everything else fades away.

12

A NEW METHOD

Academy Award winning producer, Arnold Kopelson (SEVEN, PLATOON, ERASER, THE FUGITIVE), once said that he would never make a movie unless he could see the trailer first. The following chapter aims to make that a reality.

With budgets spiraling up, costs rocketing out of control, the pandemic escalating, movies are riskier than ever. Which ones should be made? The question has become even more dire.

A new method is needed.

Scripts have traditionally been used, and they provide a decent oracle of whether the production will work or not; storyboards also aid the visualization process. But more is needed. And, thankfully, more is available. To put it plainly: **the creatives and the financiers should make the trailer before they make the movie.**

A script is needed, of course.

But beyond that, the trailer should be done before anything else—before casting, before set-building, before storyboarding.

Simply, the trailer should be the next step after the script.

The trailer, in many ways, is a superior preview to the script. It takes an entire day to read a script; it only takes two minutes to view a trailer. It's a presentation that can just be set on 'play.'

But how does one make a trailer before the film is even shot?

First, through voice over. Then, through clips from other movies.

It is done through the techniques gathered in this book.

First, the trailer producer goes through the script, looking for the appropriate lines. That would be 'exposition' and 'action.' He selects—minimum—20 lines, perhaps even more. If feeling particularly ambitious, he could select the entire script—although that is not necessary. Then he hires a series of voice over artists. Three or so would do. He gets them to record the lines of exposition and action-dialogue. If he wants to go further, if he wants to actually show the talking of the line, he could hire a model, an actor, a whatever, and a cinematographer, and then shoot the close up of that exposition or action-dialogue. It does not have to be perfect or spectacular. Just competent. It will only—potentially—be on screen for 20 or so frames.

With the recorded lines of exposition and action-dialogue, he sets about arranging them in the correct order. He uses the chapter in this book about arranging dialogue. He builds up juxtapositions and dialectics between exposition and action-dialogue, moving them back and forth, answering one another, raising questions, until, through the principles of story design, he has a compelling audio trailer.

Next, the producer layers in the rhythm. By either pre-established music or the metronome. In this case, using copyrighted music will not matter, as the trailer is not for public display. The producer might want to find the best possible music available. He lays the music down and sets the rhythm according to either the music, or the metronome.

The producer then goes through and adds in his non-diegetic sound effects, his stops, impacts, accents, and risers.

Then, the producer sets out to find five to ten movies like his.

The more the better. He goes through, recording both impact and picture-shots from all the movies. That's right. He just goes through other movies. So much money and time has already been expended in obtaining hours and hours of trailer worthy shots, it would be a shame not to use them. To save time, the trailer producer could even go through other trailers and pick shots from them.

Then, the producer overlays the arranged dialogue with the "cribbed" shots, parlaying them out according to the principles described in this book. Impact shots go after lines of dialogue, the picture shots connect the impacts.

Suddenly, a unique trailer emerges. Suddenly, a multi-million-dollar production was skipped, and now a true preview of coming attractions is had. The producer, the team involved, the executive, everyone, can truly see into the future, can see a very good approximation of how that script would have translated into a blockbuster motion picture. Was there appropriate exposition? Was there appropriate action-dialogue? It wouldn't be unusual, at this stage, for the producer to request a re-vamping of the script.

It becomes very clear, vis-a-vie this trailer, what the movie *is,* and what it needs to be.

With this trailer, everyone has a clear picture; everyone is on the same page. Unlike a script, the preview-trailer is a portable affair that can be shuttled to whomever might be interested in the movie—from the weary executive to the cautious star. Everyone can now see how well the script translates into a movie.

Or they can see how poorly it translates.

Doing this method would save countless productions the agony of venturing into the years of production on a script that was not yet ready for the trailer. Because if the trailer is the ultimate purveyor of a movie, then it's the trailer the script has to be ready for.

It is the trailer the script should be written for—not the movie.

As films become more expensive, as executives begin to see how truly temporal movies are, how little the actual quality of the film matters, how much of the discussion of the film centers around the trailer, it will be more and more necessary for all involved to project the trailer as early as possible. This method makes that available.

CONCLUSION

More movies will be made; even more trailers will need producing. The competition of media-clutter will grow denser with each day. It is through trailer production that the war for attention will be won and directed. It is through excellent trailers that any kind of movie-success will be had. Yeomen—and yeowomen—of Hollywood looking to create their own estate in the cinema-pantheon must master the craft of creating those kinds of trailers. It is one of the only direct routes to "breaking through."

It is the fastest way of being seen.

Producing a trailer, of course, is difficult, taxing work. It takes patience, diligence, creativity, and fortitude. The determination to see the final trailer, where the movie truly comes alive, unlike in any format the movie will ever come to life. Indeed, seeing the final trailer is a reward unto itself. It takes work to get there. It takes sweat and tears. It takes a review of this book. The concepts outlined will require a lot of re-reading and re-digesting. It's recommended that the trailer producer return to the pages, especially with each new challenge. Only through study will the principles in this book soak into the subconscious and ultimately aid, unabetted, the trailer producer in creating blockbuster movie trailers. The trailer producer, with this treatise, does not need to fumble about in the dark, feeling through the foibles of trial and error. He or she has a guide.

But with that comes the caveat: the work still must be done. And with every new trailer comes even newer challenges. No matter how deeply the principles of trailer design, production, are etched in stone, a new day tests their mettle. Movies creep across the desk without a story, the dialogue wasn't recorded well, no appeal can be found, there's a dearth of impacts, on and on; there are always problems. An anxiety creeps up during production for a reason. It is the trees looming down; the walls closing in. Anyone attempting to make a trailer will notice that tension around the half-way mark, perhaps even nearer the beginning. It is a mysterious tension. Of which no book can spell away.

It is up to the trailer producer, armed with the words in this book, to press on and solve each new challenge as it arises. Indeed, he or she may not want to be bothered. That is fine. It is not easy to be both filmmaker/executive/producer AND salesperson simultaneously.

If the reader would like console, would like to have the concepts of this book further clarified, would need the theories of this book to be implemented, would simply like help, please email me, Tom Getty, the author, at tgetty1@gmail.com.

I regularly create and produce movie trailers, often from scratch. That is, I usually only have the movie to work from, and no music to cut to. Music has to be invented. Indeed, a lot has to be invented. Sounds, copy, graphics, re-voicings, etc.

Trailer producers will always have to invent. Like MacGyver, the trailer producer must work with what is available. He or she must rely on their own wits, talent, and now, with a reading of this book, their education.

It is my hope that the words in this book will aid the trailer producer on his or her journey in forging out the movie trailers of tomorrow—blockbuster or not.

To the trailer producer: best of luck!

Tom Getty
January 20, 2022
Johnstown, PA

REFERENCES

Baken, R.J. *Clinical Measurement of Speech and Voice.* London: Taylor and Francis Ltd., 2000.

Collier, Robert. *The Robert Collier Letter Book.* Eastford, CT: Martino Fine Books, 2018.

Eisenstein, Sergei. *Film Form: Essays In Film Theory.* New York, NY: Harvest/HBJ, 1949.

Guttmann, A. *"U.S. Motion Picture and Videotape Production Industry Ad Spend 2020."* Statista, August 6, 2021. https://www.statista.com/statistics/470680/motion-picture-and-videotape-production-industry-ad-spend-usa/.

Hewitt, Michael. *Music Theory For Computer Muscians.* Boston, MA: Course Technology, 2008.

Itti, Laurent, and Christof Koch. *"A Saliency-Based Search Mechanism for Overt and Covert Shifts of Visual Attention."* Vision Research 40, no. 10-12 (2000): 1489–1506. https://doi.org/10.1016/s0042-6989(99)00163-7.

Kennedy, Dan S. *The Ultimate Sales Letter: Attract New Customers, Boost Your Sales.* 4th ed. Avon, MA: Adams Business, 2011.

McKee, Robert. *Dialogue: The Art of Verbal Action for Page, Stage,*

Screen. New York, NY: Twelve, 2016.

McKee, Robert. *Story: Substance, Structure, Style, and the Principles of Screenwriting.* New York, NY: Regan Books, 1997.

McWade, John. *Before & After: How To Design Cool Stuff.* Berkeley, CA, CA: Peachpit, 2010.

Metz, Christian, and Michael Taylor. *Film Language: A Semiotics of the Cinema.* Univ of Chicagoed. Chicago, IL: University of Chicago Press, 1990.

Navarro, José Gabriel. "*Expenses of the U.S. Motion Picture and Video Industries 2007-2019.*" Statista, August 12, 2021. https://www.statista.com/statistics/185312/estimated-expenses-of-us-motion-picture-and-video-industry-since-2005/.

Pepperman, Richard D., and Mark Pacella. *The Eye Is Quicker: Film Editing: Making a Good Film Better.* Studio City, CA: Michael Wiese Productions, 2004.

Rosendorf, Theodore. *The Typographic Desk Reference.* New Castle, DE: Oak Knoll Press, 2009.

Sonnenschein, David. *Sound Design: The Expressive Power of Music, Voice, and Sound Effects in Cinema.* Studio City, CA: Michael Wiese Productions, 2001.

Whitman, Drew Eric. *Cashvertising: How to Use More than 100 Secrets of Ad-Agency Psychology to Make Big Money Selling Anything to Anyone.* Franklin Lakes, NJ: Career Press, 2009.

Index

TOM GETTY

Tom Getty is a movie trailer producer, and an award-winning writer, director, and actor, known for AMERICA HAS FALLEN (2016) and EMU-LATION (2010). He attended the University of Pittsburgh and graduated *cum laude* with a degree in communications. He creates professional movie trailers for film companies around the world. He can be reached at tgetty1@gmail.com

www.ingramcontent.com/pod-product-compliance
Lightning Source LLC
LaVergne TN
LVHW021451080426
835509LV00018B/2237